THE
JUSTICE
RIDERS

A THREAT TO JUSTICE

★ A NOVEL ★

THE JUSTICE RIDERS

A THREAT TO JUSTICE

★ A NOVEL ★

CHUCK NORRIS
KEN ABRAHAM
AARON NORRIS & TIM GRAYEM

B&H PUBLISHING GROUP

NASHVILLE, TENNESSEE

ISBN: 978-0-8054-44033-1

Published by B&H Publishing Group
Nashville, Tennessee

Dewey Decimal: F
Subject Heading Classification: WESTERN STORIES \
ADVENTURE FICTION

This book is a work of fiction, intended to entertain
and inspire. Although it is loosely based on actual historical
events near the end of the American Civil War, the names,
characters, places, and incidents are the products of the
authors' imaginations. In some cases, fictitious words or
actions have been attributed to real individuals,
but these, too, are total fabrications.

1 2 3 4 5 6 7 8 9   11 10 09 08 07

Dedication

This book is dedicated to the brave men and women of the United States armed forces who are currently fighting, and have fought, for freedom and justice. Although *The Justice Riders* is based loosely on historical events, our characters are fictitious people fighting fictitious enemies in fictitious battles. But the men and women who have laid their lives on the line so we may live in peace and security are fighting real enemies in real life-or-death situations. In this small way, we honor them and thank them for being the real Justice Riders.

Chuck Norris
Aaron Norris
Tim Grayem
Ken Abraham

Acknowledgments

Many thanks to Ken Stephens, David Shepherd, Leonard Goss, Kim Overcash Stanford, Jeff Godby, Paul Mikos, and the staff and sales force of B&H Publishing Group for believing in the potential of The Justice Riders series, and for their commitment to producing an excellent product that will entertain and inspire.

Special thanks to our agent and good friend, Mark Sweeney, for encouraging us to write this story. Without Mark's confidence in us, the Justice Riders may never have "saddled up." Thanks, too, to Mike Forshey for working with Mark to iron out all our contract details. Grateful appreciation is also extended to Felix Saez of Stone Art Gallery in Park City, Utah, for his image of Chuck Norris used to depict "Ezra Justice" in the front cover art.

And thanks to our family members for putting up with us as we've worked on this project.

Most of all, thanks to the Lord Jesus Christ. He is the Ultimate Justice Rider (see Rev. 19:11).

The six heavily armed horsemen rode slowly into the town of Clinton, Missouri, their eyes scanning the periphery, searching for any sign of trouble, looking as though they were ready for a fight. Leading the pack was Captain Ezra Justice, a veteran officer in the Union Army, handpicked by General William Tecumseh Sherman to carry out covert missions against the Confederate Army during the Civil War.

Nathaniel York, a large, strong, black man rode next to Ezra. "Big Nate," as Nathaniel was known to his friends, pulled his Yankee kepi cap down farther on his head to shield his eyes from the sun, squinting to get a better look at the scene in front of them. A crowd had gathered in front of The Redheaded Lady, the town's popular watering hole.

"Look like trouble to you, Captain?" Nate asked, his eyes darting back and forth from one side of Main Street to the other.

"I don't think so," Ezra replied, sitting up straight in his saddle, eyes peering straight ahead but aware of everything around him. "Looks to me like the town has remained calm and peaceful." Captain Ezra Justice raised his right arm, and the four men following him and Nate reined their horses to a halt on the edge of town. "Let's hold up here for a moment," Justice said over his shoulder.

"I have Mr. Henry loaded and ready, Captain," Reginald Bonesteel said, patting the .44 caliber long-barreled rifle protruding from a pouch strapped on the side of his horse. "Just in case."

Justice nodded, and a faint glimmer of a smile creased his face. He knew the British-born Bonesteel was always itching for a gun battle. And with Bonesteel's outstanding marksmanship, few men stood much of a chance against him. Less than a month earlier, Bonesteel had perched atop some of Clinton's highest rooftops picking off villains and, along with the other Justice Riders, had helped free the town from the oppressive vice-like grip of Mordecai Slate's Death Raiders.

"I don't think we'll need them, but keep your guns ready," Ezra said. "Can't be too careful these days. Some soldiers on both sides are still fighting their own wars." The other men with Justice rested their hands close to their revolvers.

Carlos and Roberto Hawkins, good-looking, lighthearted twins in their mid-twenties, nudged their horses in behind Bonesteel's mount. Fresh off the streets of New York City prior to the War between the States, Carlos and Roberto had matured quickly through the rigors of battle. Their clever exploits with explosives had established them as legends among surviving soldiers, and the stories of their bold, death-defying antics grew ever more outlandish with each retelling.

Next to the twins rode the tall, muscular Harry Whitecloud, the son of a Sioux woman and a white man. Harry went by his mother's maiden name because his father had deserted the family while his mother was still pregnant with Harry. Harry's long black hair and his ruddy skin tone highlighted his finely chiseled facial features, reflecting his mother's heritage. Harry had lived off the land among the Indians, learning the mystic healing arts of the medicine man. But he wanted to study modern medicine, so he applied to and was accepted at Princeton. That's where he was located at the outbreak of war, so he joined the Union forces at Philadelphia. A fearless warrior, Harry could do things with a bowie knife that even skilled hunters only dreamed about. And his tracking abilities were the best in the Federal army.

Together the six men had worked under the direct commission of General William Tecumseh Sherman, wreaking havoc among Confederate troops and hastening the end of the war through their courageous, unorthodox methods of sabotage and destruction. Soldiers on both sides of the Mason-Dixon Line had learned to respect the group known as the Justice Riders.

They had just left the home of Elizabeth O'Banyon, where they had buried the seventh man in their small contingency, Shaun O'Banyon. Shaun had sacrificed his life to help save the lives of the other Justice Riders. With his dying breath, he had asked Justice to take him home to his wife, Lizzie, for burial;

and at great risk to themselves, the Riders had fulfilled the last request of their fellow soldier.

Now the war was over, and the Justice Riders looked forward to a time of peace and reconstruction in the reunited country. They were ready to strike out on their own individual adventures: some in search of fortunes; others looking for new challenges; others, like Ezra and Nate, were hoping to reestablish something of life as they knew it back in Tennessee before the war. The Justice Riders were making one final sweep through Clinton to make sure everything was back to normal before they headed off on their own pursuits. They also had received word from the Clinton bank that their back pay had finally arrived.

Now that the Justice Riders had destroyed Mordecai Slate's rogue gang of malcontents known as the Death Raiders, Ezra had felt free to contact General Sherman to inform him that the Justice Riders' mission was complete. In a telegram message to General Sherman, Justice told his commanding officer: "Shaun O'Banyon delivered. Mordecai Slate's gang destroyed. Mission accomplished."

Ezra had earlier telegraphed General Sherman, requesting that the army pay the Justice Riders their six months of back pay. Justice suggested that the army could send the back pay to the Clinton bank, and the men could pick it up there, subtly letting General Sherman know that the Justice Riders would soon be going their separate ways.

General Sherman responded promptly, promising to contact the bank so the Justice Riders could receive their pay.

BEFORE THE JUSTICE RIDERS left Elizabeth O'Banyon's farm and proceeded on their way back toward Clinton, they had casually talked about their future plans. British-born Reginald Bonesteel planned to go west, hoping to make a fortune in the newly discovered gold fields of northern California. Harry Whitecloud planned to go back to the university to pursue his medical studies and one day move back to the Sioux reservation to help his people. The Hawkins twins longed for exciting adventures and hoped to find them in St. Louis or perhaps in New Orleans. Ezra and Nate planned to return to the Justice family plantation in Tennessee—if there was anything left of it.

"Everybody ready?" Ezra asked, knowing the answer before he asked. "Alright, let's go." Ezra led the way up Main Street. As Ezra Justice and his men rode slowly into Clinton, they were not prepared for what greeted them. Men, women, and children alike poured out onto the town's boardwalk and began to cheer and applaud. Some of the children fell into line alongside and behind the Justice Riders, forming a spontaneous parade through the center of town.

"Wow, Ezra! They sure are happy to see us!" Nate said.

"Yeah, they are able to walk the streets safely again," Ezra replied. The Justice Riders continued riding toward the bank. Ezra slowly raised his hand to acknowledge some of the men along the boardwalk. Seeing the response from Ezra Justice, the men began calling out words of thanks and gratitude to the

Justice Riders, and the cheering increased. The Justice Riders slowly made their way up the street, the crowd growing larger, with more and more people following behind the six soldiers.

"Welcome back," one man called from the crowd.

"Sure hope you plan on staying!" someone else called out. "Our town is your town. We can't thank you enough!"

The adulation of the townsfolk caused Ezra to feel a bit uncomfortable. He appreciated the many kind comments of the people, but as far as he was concerned, he and his men had simply done their jobs in ridding the town of Slate and his evil gang.

They rode up to the bank where the army paymaster had sent their back pay. When Ezra and his men dismounted, the crowd gathered around and cheered as though the Justice Riders were favorite sons coming home after the war, the men shaking their hands and slapping the Justice Riders on their backs, the women nodding their appreciation, and some of them even hugging and kissing the Justice Riders on their cheeks.

"Oh, thank you for what you did for us," one woman gushed. "You saved our town."

Not usually one for speeches, Ezra felt compelled to say something. He stood on the boardwalk in front of the bank and addressed the crowd.

"Less than a month ago, this town was under siege by a ruthless gang of misguided gunslingers, following the lead of a truly evil man," Ezra said. "But with God's help and yours, we faced them down and wiped them out. Freedom is your right; don't ever let anyone take that away from you again."

"We won't, Captain!" a man called out from the crowd.

"Never again!" another agreed. The crowd erupted in applause. Ezra tamped his hands and arms toward the ground, trying to quiet the cheers. He looked over at the other Justice Riders, who were standing behind him in front of the bank. The cheering continued, so Carlos and Roberto took off their hats and waved them to the people in the crowd; Reginald Boneteel, Nathaniel York, and Harry Whitecloud removed their caps and simply nodded.

"I'm not one for long-winded speeches, so I'll just say this and be done. It's time for my men and me to move on." A collective sigh swept over the crowd, followed by a hush as Ezra continued. "We've made some good friends here, so don't be surprised if you see us come back from time to time. But until then, keep freedom alive and don't let any threat to justice stand." Ezra tipped his hat to the people and said, "Thank you, folks, for this kind reception. May God bless you. Good-bye."

The crowd broke into loud applause and cheers once again as the Justice Riders waved their hats high in the air, then replaced them, turned around, and walked inside the bank.

Amos Smithson, the bank manager, had been watching and listening to the commotion through his window. He slid his spectacles higher on his nose and hurried to greet Ezra and the men as they came though the door. "Good afternoon, gentlemen," he said, reaching out his hand to Ezra. "And welcome back to Clinton. I'm Amos Smithson, the manager here at First National. We've been expecting you. As you can tell, the folks of this town are greatly indebted to you and are much appreciative of your . . . er . . . ah, shall we say, your *talents*." Smithson eyed the large LaMat revolver strapped to Ezra's thigh.

"Thank you, Mr. Smithson," Ezra replied. "We won't keep you long. We received your message saying that General Sherman's package had arrived for us."

"That's right, Captain," Smithson said. "Your back pay is here. We have already counted it out and prepared the individual payments for you, but allow me to double-check each one to make sure the amounts are correct.

"Please step right over here to the tellers' windows," Mr. Smithson said, "and I'll get the money out of the safe and distribute it."

As Amos Smithson counted out the cash for each of the Justice Riders, their eyes got wider and wider. "That's more than six months of pay!" Carlos said to Roberto.

The bank manager looked up and smiled but kept counting. "The letter here says to pay each of you a thousand dollars," Mr. Smithson said. "The letter is from General Sherman. And it says, 'Job well-done.'"

"Hot diggidies! We're going to have a great time in New Orleans with all this money!" Carlos crowed.

"If we don't spend it all in St. Louis," Roberto added.

Ezra Justice was the last member of the group to receive his back pay. "I'll be paying you double, Captain Justice," the bank manager said. "My instructions are to give you the pay belonging to Sergeant Shaun O'Banyon, as well."

"I understand," Justice replied. "That will be just fine." After Ezra received his and O'Banyon's pay, he turned to his men and said, "Nate and I will drop off Shaun's portion to Elizabeth on the way out of town."

"That's a good idea," Reginald Bonesteel said. "No doubt, it will be a pleasant surprise to her."

"More than that, Reginald. This money will be a great blessing to Mrs. O'Banyon," Nathaniel York said. "She can now hire someone to help with the farm. Lord knows she can sure use the help."

His job complete, Amos Smithson came back out from behind the bank counter. "I just want to add my thanks, Mr. Justice, for all that you and your men did to set our town free. Before you showed up, I was afraid to open the bank for business because those Death Raiders were always around. Nobody had the courage to challenge them, so they pretty much took whatever they wanted—food, drinks, some of our women, and a lot of our money. This town would have died had it not been for you men."

"Bullies will always be around, Mr. Smithson," Nate said. "The faces change, but the hearts are the same. They'll try to get away with as much as they can. But if good people will stand up to them and say, 'That's enough,' the bullies can easily be beaten."

"Well, I don't know about that," Smithson said, "but I sure appreciate your courage and willingness to stand up for what is right."

"Thank you, Mr. Smithson." Ezra nodded. "You take care now."

"Oh, I will," Smithson said. "You men do the same."

"We will," Ezra replied. Ezra and his men filed out of the bank.

Once outside the door, Nate nudged Ezra in the ribs. "Take care? You ain't never taken care in all your life, Ezra Justice."

Ezra almost smiled. "Well, Nate, some people like to take care, and others like to take charge. I figured Mr. Smithson would rather take care."

The men continued counting their money as they headed for the general store to get some supplies, ready to strike out in search of their fortunes . . . or misfortunes.

After everyone had purchased the items they wanted and packed them onto their horses, there was no longer a reason to stay, but Roberto Hawkins didn't want to see the group disband. "Before we all go off in various directions, let's have one final drink together," Roberto suggested.

"You do come up with a good idea once in a great while, little brother," Carlos said. Everyone laughed as the men tied up their horses in front of The Redheaded Lady saloon and stepped inside. The saloon was busy, especially for late afternoon, and when the men inside recognized the Justice Riders, another spontaneous cheer broke out.

"I'd like a round of drinks for our men," Harry Whitecloud said to Joe Thompson, the stout, bearded, apron-clad bartender.

"No sirrie, today the drinks are on me," Joe said as Harry Whitecloud tried to hand him some money to pay for the drinks.

"We can well afford to pay you, Joe," Harry Whitecloud said, pushing the money across the bar toward the cash register.

Joe pushed the money back toward Harry. "Mordecai Slate and his men just about put me out of business," Joe said, "and would have if it hadn't been for you men." The bartender shook his head as he spoke as though trying to shake off a nightmarish thought. "So today it is my privilege to offer the Justice Riders anything you want to drink, to show my appreciation."

"Here, here!" several men in the bar shouted, as they raised their glasses high in the air in a salute to the Justice Riders.

Ezra Justice and his men stayed for a short while, talking with the men of Clinton, reliving some of the escapades of the Justice Riders, recalling the ferocious life-or-death gun battle between the Justice Riders and the Death Raiders and the personal duel between villainous Mordecai Slate and Ezra Justice in which Justice felled Slate with one shot. The Justice Riders relished the kind words of the well-wishers and felt reluctant to leave, yet they knew the time was rapidly approaching for their departure.

After they had their drink, Ezra and his men left the saloon and walked outside to their horses. As they prepared to mount, the men who had lived together for more than a year before the end of the Civil War—eating, sleeping, fighting the enemy, watching out for one another every day and night—looked at each other awkwardly, not knowing what to say.

"This is strange," Carlos said, shaking his head. "We've been locked at the hips for the past year, depending on one another and defending one another with our lives. It's tough just to say good-bye and walk away." The men fell into a heavy silence, pretending to be cinching their saddles tighter, placing items in their saddlebags, or checking their horses' hooves for stones. For the first time since they had met, they shared an odd uneasiness.

Ezra finally broke the silence. "Remember, men; just as we agreed before we left Elizabeth O'Banyon's place, if any of you ever need me, just contact Elizabeth; I'll keep in touch with her, and she will know how to reach me."

"That goes for me, too," said Reginald Bonesteel.

The others chimed in with, "Same here; me, too!"

"Alright, let's agree; keep Elizabeth aware of your where-abouts so if any of us are needed, we can be contacted quickly through her. When Nate and I drop the money off with her, I will remind her about our arrangement."

As everyone was shaking hands and hugging, a man from the telegraph office came running up. "Captain Justice! Mr. Justice," he called out as he approached.

"This just came in from Washington, sir," he said, waving a telegram toward Ezra. "The salutation said it was urgent."

"Thank you," Ezra said, as he took the telegram from the messenger's hands.

"Urgent, hmmm. I don't like the feeling of this," Ezra said, looking at the telegram. He stood staring at the important message in his hands.

Nate raised his eyebrows and said, "Are you going to open it?"

"I don't know if I want to . . ."

"You gotta open it, Captain Justice," Carlos Hawkins howled. "Maybe you inherited a fortune or something."

"Or maybe the law finally caught up with you two hooligans," Bonesteel deadpanned in the direction of the Hawkins twins.

"I think he just insulted us, Roberto," Carlos said, pretending that his feelings were hurt.

"Nah, you have to care about the opinion of someone before he can insult you," Roberto quipped. Ezra Justice ignored the playful repartee between his soldiers.

"Maybe the army is reassigning us," Harry Whitecloud suggested. "Would that be possible?"

"Well, there's only one way to find out, Harry," Justice answered as he tore open the envelope. "Now that the war is over, most men are mustering out. You'd have to make a special effort to stay in the army. Most soldiers are looking forward to going home and getting back to work." Ezra's eyes scanned the telegram in his hand, slowly shaking his head as he read it. "Everyone except us, I guess."

"What do you mean? What does it say, Captain?" Carlos asked.

"It's from General Sherman," Ezra said slowly, the surprise obvious in his voice, "and he is summoning us to Washington, as soon as possible."

"Washington? I'm planning to spend some time in St. Louis," Roberto blurted.

"Yeah, me too," said Carlos. "I hear there are lots of pretty women in St. Louis, all looking for just the right man."

"So pray tell, my man, why would you be going there?" Bonesteel said. Ezra continued to ignore the banter between his soldiers as he read the telegram again, just to make sure he hadn't missed anything.

"It looks as though our orders have been changed," Ezra continued. "General Sherman wants us to report to him in Washington before we go our separate ways. He says it is a matter of utmost importance." Ezra read part of the telegram aloud to the others:

> *"To Captain Ezra Justice and the Justice Riders.*
> *Return to Washington as soon as possible. There are*
> *matters of utmost importance to discuss."*

Ezra rubbed his chin. "What could possibly be more important than getting back home and restarting our lives?"

"Wait a minute," said Carlos. "We just got all this money! And me and my brother are itching to spend it, beginning in St. Louis and then in New Orleans—if we have any money left that is, after we've spent some time in St. Louis. Is this an optional trip, Captain?"

"You tell me, Carlos," Ezra said. "I haven't finished reading the telegram yet. The General also says that if we don't show up, he will hunt us down and skin us alive!"

"Oh," said Carlos, his countenance drooping. "That answers my question."

"Well, we'd better get going then," said Nate. "I don't look to being skinned by the General."

"Are we really required to go, Captain?" Harry Whitecloud asked seriously.

Ezra waved the yellow telegram in front of him. "It is a command, Harry," Justice said, "not a suggestion. As long as we are still in the army, we have to obey. Disobedience of a direct command could be costly."

"I understand, Captain," Whitecloud replied.

"What do you think we should do, Ezra?" Nate asked.

"Let's head on up to Jefferson City, which is the next big town where we can replenish our supplies again for the trip. It's a long way to Washington, even if we can catch some trains along the way. We'll go to Washington, meet with General Sherman, and then we can all go our separate ways from there."

"Hmm, Washington, you say," Bonesteel said thoughtfully. "Fine dining, sophisticated female company, and afternoon teas. Wonderful." The stately Brit tilted his head back and looked to the sky as he spoke. "Perhaps I should retrieve my uniform from West Point, the one I wore when I was still with the Queen's Coldstream Guard."

"Ha! That silly plumed hat that stood about two feet tall?" Carlos hooted. "The soldiers in Sherman's ranks will think you are forming a marching band or something. Forget it, Reginald. You're one of us now—not that I wouldn't enjoy seeing you in that stuffy British dress uniform again, with all the brass buttons and sashes. I could use a good laugh!"

"Why you . . ." Bonesteel looked as though he was ready to dismount and take after Carlos.

"Let's be on our way, men," said Justice. "We have a long journey."

BEFORE LEAVING CLINTON, the Justice Riders returned to the O'Banyon farm to give Elizabeth her husband Shaun's back pay. As the Justice Riders approached the house, Elizabeth walked out on the front porch. "Back already? Looks like you boys just can't live without me," she said with a smile.

Ezra responded, "Elizabeth, we do think a lot of you, but we're not staying. Our reason for returning is simply to give you Shaun's back pay of one thousand dollars." Ezra dismounted and handed a bag of money to Elizabeth.

"One thousand dollars!" Elizabeth placed her hand over her heart. "Oh, thank you, Ezra; this money will go a long way in keeping up this farm. Now I can afford to hire some help."

"Don't thank us; thank General Sherman for being so generous."

The Justice Riders reminded Elizabeth that they would keep in touch, and she agreed to be the conduit through which information about the other men could flow. They said their good-byes once again, and the Justice Riders galloped off toward the east to find out what was so urgent that General Sherman would ask them to return to the Capitol.

For several days the Justice Riders kept a grueling pace, traversing mile after mile of rugged terrain as they made their way to Jefferson City. It was almost dusk when they arrived in town. Ezra and Nate headed for the general store, hoping to get there before it closed, while the other men steered straight for the saloon, tying up their horses at the rail running along the boardwalk in front of the local watering hole. "Let us know if you need some help there, Captain," Roberto called.

"We can handle it," Justice answered. Ezra and Nate continued up the street and dismounted in front of the supply store. They tied their horses to the hitching post and disappeared inside the building.

Reginald Bonesteel and Harry Whitecloud entered the bustling saloon first; they stepped past the bar and found an available table near the back corner of the lantern-lit room.

"Might you have a spot of tea?" Bonesteel asked a saloon girl passing by.

"Tea?" She looked at him quizzically. "I can brew up some coffee if you'd like, but tea? My grandma makes delicious sweet tea at home, but I ain't never seen the likes served in here."

"Two cups of coffee will be fine," Harry Whitecloud said, slapping Bonesteel on the back as the two men sat down at the table.

The Hawkins twins followed behind them but never made it to the table. They spied a poker game near the front of the room, and they immediately approached the four men seated around the table.

"Got room for two more?" Roberto asked.

"Yeah, if you got money to lose," a burly fellow said.

"Sure, we got lots of money," Carlos bragged. "But we don't plan on losing it."

"We'll see about that, young fella. I've been pounding spikes in the railroad ties going across High Bridge all day, and I am ready to clean up on some Yankee prima donnas."

Roberto smiled and stretched out his hand. "Roberto Hawkins, certified Yankee prima donna," he joked, shaking hands with the big burly fellow. "This is my brother, Carlos. We're just passing through town on our way east and looking for a little action."

"You've come to the right place, Yankees. Have a seat." The big man passed the deck of cards to Roberto. "Why don't you deal, Roberto?"

"Seems to me that Missouri was on the side of the Federals during the war, wasn't it?" Roberto said as he took the cards and began to shuffle.

"Some of us were, and some of us weren't. My family was from Alabama, right near Cahaba. Ever hear of that?"

"Oh, yeah, we know about Cahaba," Roberto replied. Images of the horrific Confederate prisoner of war camp that the Justice Riders had helped liberate just a few months earlier flitted through Roberto's mind. Roberto had never seen men treat one another so cruelly as the Yankee prisoners had been treated in the camps at Cahaba, Alabama, and Andersonville, Georgia.

"Yeah, I was a prison guard there for the last fifteen months of the war," the big man said as he spat some tobacco juice on the floor.

"Were you happy about that?" Roberto asked.

"No, I wasn't happy about it, Yankee. I was just doing my job."

TWO PRETTY SALOON GIRLS, Jenny and Eva, noticed the handsome Hawkins brothers seated at the poker table and sashayed in the twins' direction, flirting with their eyes, their body language sending unmistakably seductive messages. Tan-skinned and petite, Jenny looked to be about twenty years of age, her curly, long brown hair swirling down around her shoulders, her dress highlighting her figure, pinched at the waist and slightly flared at the bottom.

Eva, the older woman, flipped her straight blonde hair over her back, the low-cut dress allowing more than a little of her bare, white shoulders to be exposed to the Hawkins twins.

"Whoowee!" Carlos whistled under his breath to Roberto. "Get a load of that!"

"Keep your mind on your cards," Roberto said loudly, making no effort to conceal his comment.

The women were equally as overt as they sidled up next to Carlos and Roberto, Jenny to the left of Carlos, and Eva to the right of Roberto.

"Nice hand," Eva said, looking down at Roberto's hand covering his cards. "Bet you have some good cards in there, too. Mind if we join you, gentlemen?" Eva said with a friendly smile.

"Hmph. Gentlemen," the big local man grunted. "I'll bet."

"Yes, we'll be your good-luck charms," Jenny said as she put her arm around Carlos's neck and in one flowing motion swung around onto his lap.

"Whoa, girl!" Carlos said with a surprised laugh, his cards nearly flying out of his left hand. His right arm instinctively went around Jenny and caught her shoulders as she leaned back against him. "I think my luck has gotten better already!"

Eva pulled a chair alongside Roberto and sat down facing him, her back to the poker player to Roberto's right. She crossed her legs, leaned forward, and looked at the cards

Roberto was holding. She smiled playfully at him and said, "Ready to fold?"

Roberto returned Eva's smile and winked at her. "If you mean these cards, yes I am. But we just got started. Let me make some money here, pretty lady, and maybe you and I will take some time to get to know each other better. In the meantime stay close to me. A lovely lady such as you shouldn't be alone in a place like this. Can I get you something to drink?"

"Well, thank you . . . er . . ."

"Roberto. Roberto Hawkins, and that's my brother, Carlos."

"Why, thank you, Roberto Hawkins," Eva said, "but actually, I'm supposed to be asking you that question. Jenny and I—I'm Eva—we work here."

"You are working here?" Roberto exclaimed. "A fine woman like yourself? I thought certainly that you must be a guest at the hotel across the street. You look so cultured and refined; your sophistication shines in your face. My! The war must have taken a toll on you, didn't it? I guess it did on all of us. But it did nothing to detract from your beauty, Eva."

It had been a long time since Eva had blushed, yet she suddenly felt the blood rushing uncontrollably to her cheeks. "Why, thank you, Roberto." She lightly patted her face, now a bright pink. "You do know how to make a girl feel like a lady, now don't you?"

"Yes, ma'am. You look like a fine lady to me. We've all been through some tough times these past few years. It doesn't mean that is where we have to stay in our lives. I'm heading for St. Louis before long myself."

"St. Louis?" Eva repeated with a nod and a faraway look in her eyes. "That's as good a place as any to start over, I suppose."

Just then, several ranch hands burst noisily through the swinging doors of the saloon. Slapping one another on the back and shouting obscenities, they approached the bar. "Whiskey!" one of the men shouted.

"Not for me, Ben," another shouted. "It was hot as Hades out there on the ranch today. Give me something cold to drink."

"Give me whiskey, Ben, and lots of it," Jake Stone called.

Benjamin Jones, the bartender, hurriedly scrambled to fill the men's glasses with their favorite drinks.

"Hurry up, Ben," Jake hollered again. "I'm about to die of thirst."

"I'm hurrying, Jake," Ben answered. "Can't you see that I have a lot of customers tonight?"

Jake slapped his hand down on the bar, making a loud cracking sound and sending several glasses crashing to the floor. In the far corner of the room, Harry Whitecloud's senses perked up, as did those of Reginald Bonesteel. The Hawkins twins were having too much fun to notice.

"Bring me a bottle of whiskey, Ben!" Jake Stone bellowed again. "My friends up in the hills out of town got plenty of moonshine. But who wants that joy juice? My boys and me have been out there branding cattle all day long, and we want to have some fun tonight. Right, boys?"

"That's right, Jake."

As Jake poured whiskey into their glasses, the ranch hands downed several drinks in succession, growing more belligerent with each belt. "Another bottle, Ben!" Jake called.

A BURST OF LAUGHTER from the table in the front of the room—the one where the poker game was going on—caught Jake Stone's attention. He turned around, leaned back on the bar, and took another swig from his bottle. That's when he spotted Jenny sitting in Carlos Hawkins's lap, her arm around his neck, her head thrown back in laughter, her brilliant brown eyes sparkling in the dim light. Eva and the others around the table were laughing, too, although Jake couldn't see what was so funny.

"Jenny!" Jake shouted.

She either didn't hear or didn't want to hear because she paid no attention to Jake's harsh voice.

"Jenny! Get off that man and come over here."

This time Jenny heard Jake. She waved her hand from side to side in front of her face and shook her head.

"Get over here, Jenny. I want to buy you a drink!" Jake bellowed.

Jenny had worked in the bar long enough to know how to sense trouble and how to diffuse it as well. "Not right now, Jake," she called back to him sweetly. "I'm having a good time right here. You go on and have a few more drinks with your friends, and I'll have one with you later."

"I didn't ask you, Jenny. I said get yourself off that man and get over here before I come over there after you."

"And I believe you heard me when I said no, Jake. Do you know what the word means? I know it's a big one, but maybe you're bright enough to figure it out."

Jake Stone stormed across the room and grabbed Jenny by the shoulder while she was still sitting on Carlos's lap. Jenny grimaced in pain at Jake's strong grip.

Still smiling, Carlos looked up and saw Jake looming above him with his hand squeezing Jenny's shoulder. With one swat of his arm, Carlos knocked Jake's hand away from Jenny. "Easy, cowboy," Carlos said, with a winsome smile. "We're all just having some fun here."

Stone looked at Carlos and growled, "Stay out of this, stranger, if you know what's good for you."

Jenny's brown eyes were blazing. "Jake Stone, don't you ever grab me like that again," she said defiantly. "You don't own me."

"Ha!" Jake guffawed. "I don't own you, huh? You don't say!" Jake slapped Jenny across the face. She flew out of Carlos's lap, landing hard on the floor, curling up in pain, crying.

Carlos was already swinging as he came out of his chair. His fist connected squarely to Stone's big jaw, sending the cow puncher stumbling across the room, tripping over a chair, and tumbling to the floor. Carlos stood at the card table. "How does it feel, big man?" Carlos glowered. "Doesn't feel so good, does it?"

Jake Stone slowly pulled himself off the floor, glaring at Carlos, as he said, "You made a big mistake, mister." With lightning speed, Stone went for his gun, but before he could even clear leather, Carlos had beaten him to the draw and had his revolver pointed at Stone's heart.

"You're the one who nearly made a fatal mistake, my friend," Carlos said. "Now drop the gun."

Jake Stone slowly released his grip on the gun and allowed it to drop toward the saloon floor.

"And now, Mr. Jake," Carlos said, "you have a choice to make here. You can go back to your friends and continue your drinking peacefully, or we can continue our discussion with our fists."

Jake Stone grinned. "I've never been beaten in a fist fight, so if you are stupid enough to put that gun away, I'll show you why."

Carlos handed his revolver to Roberto as he said to Stone, "Well, then, it's about time you had a whippin'."

Jake Stone charged at him, throwing a vicious punch toward Carlos's face. Almost like a ghost Carlos eluded the punch. He sidestepped Stone's charge, grabbed his arm, and flipped Stone over the poker table, sending chips, drinks, and players scattering.

Carlos quickly reached down, pulled Jake up by the hair, and peppered him with a combination of rapid, powerful punches to the face. Carlos let Stone drop to the floor again and stood back, waiting to see if the big man was going to get up.

He didn't have to wait long. Stone stood, shook off the punches, and stepped toward Carlos, much more cautiously this time. Jake countered with several strong punches of his own, connecting at least twice with Carlos's face, making loud smacking sounds.

As they stood along the bar, watching the fight, Roberto said to Reginald Bonesteel, "Ouch, that will hurt tomorrow."

Several other cowhands stood along the bar, urging on their friend. "Get him, Jake. Don't let him do that to you!"

As the fight turned completely one-sided in Carlos's favor, one of Jake's friends slowly moved his hand toward his gun. Just when he saw Jake getting the worst of it, the cowpoke started to draw.

Harry Whitecloud was standing next to Jake's friend, nonchalantly watching the fracas. Before Jake's friend could get his gun waist high, Harry whirled around and pressed a large bowie knife against the man's throat. "I don't think I would do that, if I were you," Whitecloud said quietly to Stone's friend. "Just put it back in your holster, and let boys be boys."

The cowpoke's skin showed a slight dot of blood where Whitecloud's knife rested against his neck.

"Put the gun down, Sam," another man standing nearby yelled. "Jake asked for it; now let him take the licking he deserves."

"That's extremely good advice," Whitecloud said as he pressed the knife a bit harder. A couple drops of bright red blood dripped down the knife blade and fell to the floor.

"Aw, I guess you're right." Jake's friend reholstered his gun. He clutched his throat where the knife had pricked his skin, wiping the blood on his bandanna.

"Enjoy the remainder of the fight, my friend," Harry Whitecloud said with a nod.

By now Carlos was mopping the floor with Jake Stone. Just as Carlos was about to finish him off with one last, well-placed punch, Jake wobbled precariously, tumbled over a table, and landed facedown on the floor, unable to get up.

Just then a well-dressed man wearing a gray business suit and vest, cowboy boots, and a large cowboy hat, walked through the saloon doors. It was J. T. Brennen, the owner of the ranch on which Jake Stone and his men were employed.

"Mr. Brennen, how are you tonight?" Ben the bartender called out to the obviously well-to-do gentleman.

"What's going on here?" Brennen asked angrily.

"Jake brought it on himself, Mr. Brennen," Ben explained. "He tried to bully the wrong man this time. The little dark-haired guy has taken Jake apart. Not to mention taking apart most of my saloon."

"Alright, Ben," Brennen said. "Send me the damages, and Jake can pay for them out of his wages." Brennen turned to several of his men standing nearby. "Pick him up, and get him back to the ranch. The party's over!" The sophisticated gentleman whirled around on his heel and walked out of the saloon. His cowhands quickly set about the formidable task of getting Jake off the floor and into a chair so they could dump some water on his head.

EZRA JUSTICE AND NATHANIEL YORK stepped up onto the boardwalk in front of the saloon just as several cowpunchers trudged out through the doors, two of the cowboys half carrying a third man with his arms around their shoulders.

Nate stepped aside and looked at the big man, bruises already forming on his face and blood semi-congealed on several cuts above his eye. His nose looked as though it had been crushed and stuck on sideways. Nate raised his eyebrows as the men passed by. "My guess is that he got those bruises from Roberto Hawkins," Nate said to Ezra.

"Nah, it looks like Carlos's work to me," Justice replied.

"A dollar says I'm right," Nate challenged.

"Alright, you're on."

Ezra and Nate walked inside the saloon and looked around. Over in the corner they spied Roberto Hawkins congratulating his bruised but happy brother Carlos. Eva and Jenny, the saloon girls, dipped a towel into a pan of water and wiped some blood off Carlos's face. Ezra and Nate couldn't tell if the blood belonged to Carlos or had come from the big bruiser they had seen being helped out of the saloon.

Nate looked at Roberto, then at Carlos, put his hand in pocket, and pulled out a dollar. He handed it to Ezra. "Here's your dollar, Cap'n."

"You can keep your dollar, Nate. I cheated."

"Cheated? How?" said Nate.

"I could tell by the bruises on the left side of the fellow's face that he'd messed with the wrong Hawkins twin. Carlos has a deadly left hook. That cowpuncher is lucky Carlos didn't take his head off."

"I know that's the truth," Nate said, as he and Ezra walked over to Carlos.

Jenny was wiping blood from a cut above Carlos's eye.

"Evenin', ma'am. Thanks for taking care of our friend here. I just hate that he got beat up so badly. That fellow must have really whipped him good."

"Yeah, that's too bad, Carlos," Nate said, shaking his head. "Must have been that big fellow walking out of the saloon with all of his friends, laughing!"

Carlos couldn't stand it any more. He leaped out of the chair where he'd been sitting while Jenny had been attending to him. "I'll have you fellows know that I beat the tar out of that man. I'm fine, look at me. He barely touched me."

Bonesteel and Whitecloud joined Ezra, Nate, and Roberto in teasing Carlos. "Harry, we may need your medical expertise here. What do you think?" Bonesteel feigned a serious look as though he were concerned about the cut above Carlos's eye.

"It does look quite deep," Harry said, pulling out his bowie. "We may need to clean it out a bit before we sew him up. Does anyone have any rawhide?" He looked at Eva. "Is there somewhere I can sterilize my knife?"

"Hmm, I don't know, Harry. It sure looks like a lot of blood to me," Ezra said. "Are you sure you're OK, Carlos?"

"OK? Of course, I'm better than OK. I mean, yes, sir, Captain Justice. I'm perfectly fine."

"Oh, well, good. Then you won't have any problem cleaning up this mess you made." Ezra waved his arm in an arc as he perused the saloon tables in shambles. "We'll be waiting for you outside. And don't be too long; we still have a long trip ahead of us."

The Justice Riders continued their eastward trek, heading toward Eureka, Missouri. "We'll go by horseback up through St. Louis," Ezra Justice informed his men, "and catch the train there for most of the remaining journey to Washington. That will save us a lot of time."

MEANWHILE, A COVERED WAGON, pulling a horse and a milk cow behind it, slowly rumbled into the dusty town of Eureka. The wagon pulled up in front of a supply store. "Whoa," called out a ruggedly handsome man in his mid-forties, sitting on the front seat of the wagon along with a simply dressed woman. Pastor Octavius Bennett and his wife, Mildred, stepped down from the wagon. A devout man, Pastor Bennett possessed a wealth of experience as a minister, having established several congregations on the American frontier and more recently building a large church in the Chicago area. He and his family were moving from Chicago to take a new assignment in St. Louis.

Suddenly three teenage girls jumped off the back of the wagon—Ruth, fifteen years of age, spontaneous and extremely sensitive; sixteen-year-old Sara, the adventurous daughter; and the mother hen, Mary, who had recently turned seventeen. As Pastor Bennett and his wife stepped up onto the boardwalk, preparing to go into the supply store, Sara called out, "Papa, may we walk through town and look in the windows? It's been such a long time since I've seen a new dress. And Mary noticed a candle shop down the street as we came into town."

Pastor Bennett smiled, knowing that his daughters enjoyed window-shopping as much as anything. "Sure, that will be fine," he said, "but don't wander off too far because we won't be staying here long. We'll be continuing our journey to St. Louis as soon as we get our supplies."

"Oh, thank you, Papa," Sara crowed. "We'll be back shortly." The three pretty girls walked excitedly down the boardwalk, looking in the windows of each shop as they strolled.

They were barely gone when three local thugs stumbled out of the saloon, each of them carrying a bottle of whiskey in his hands. The dirty, disheveled, unshaven men spotted the three young women looking in the store windows.

"Look at that, boys, one little filly for each of us," one of the men said, smacking his lips loudly as though salivating over a good meal. They all laughed as they ambled up to the unsuspecting girls. "Hey, little ladies, would you like to have a drink with us? Or maybe you're looking for a little more action than just looking in windows."

"No, sir," Mary said, immediately protective of her younger sisters. "We are merely looking in the shop windows until our folks get supplies so we can continue our journey to St. Louis."

"Oh, that's too bad," one of the gritty looking men said with feigned sadness in his voice. "Well, since you don't have time for some fun, how about a good-bye kiss before you go back to your mommy and daddy?"

The three drunken men reached for the young ladies, trying to kiss them.

"Get away from us, please!" Sara cried.

"Take your filthy hands off me," Mary said more sternly, swatting at the hands of the man who had grabbed her shoulders.

Ruth began screaming as she tried to fight off the lecherous man pawing at her dress. She turned her face to avoid his whiskey breath and his foul mouth.

Suddenly a voice boomed, "That's enough!"

The three men turned around to see Sheriff Peter Jenkins standing there, his hands on his hips. One of the men said, "We didn't mean any harm, Sheriff. We were just having a little fun with these young ladies."

"Well, get back to the saloon and have your fun there."

"Right, Sheriff. We'll do just that."

The three thugs released the girls and hurried back to the saloon, slapping one another on the back and laughing uproariously as they went.

Mary, Sara, and Ruth were so traumatized by the brazen attack that they couldn't move. They stood huddled on the boardwalk in front of the sheriff. When he was certain the three men were inside the saloon, Sheriff Jenkins turned his attention to the Bennett daughters. "I don't recognize you girls," he said, eying the young women curiously but kindly. "Where are you from?"

"We're from Chicago," Mary said, "and we are on our way to St. Louis along with our parents, to help open a new church."

"Oh, I see. Your father is a pastor?"

"Yes, sir. He and our mom are in the store getting supplies," Sara informed Sheriff Jenkins.

"Well, now," the sheriff said. "Allow me to escort you young ladies back to the store. Even though I don't think you will be bothered anymore, it is not wise to be out on the streets without an escort."

"Thank you, sir," Mary said. "That is kind of you."

Sheriff Jenkins escorted the girls to the store, stopping out front just as the Bennetts walked out with an armload of supplies.

"Good afternoon, Reverend; Ma'am." The sheriff took off his hat and nodded toward Mrs. Bennett. "I'm Sheriff Peter Jenkins, the law around here, and apparently your daughters ran into some trouble with the local scum."

"Yeah, Mommy, they were trying to kiss us!" said Ruth.

"What?" asked Pastor Bennett, placing some packages in the covered wagon. "What's that you say about men trying to kiss you?"

Jenkins nodded toward Pastor Bennett. "What's done is done," the sheriff said. "I'd suggest you folks get your supplies packed and get along on your journey."

"Did they hurt you?" Pastor Bennett looked from one daughter to the next. "Did they touch you?"

"We're OK, Daddy," Mary said. "We were just scared."

"Thank you, Sheriff, for protecting our girls," Mildred Bennett said, wrapping Ruth in her arms.

"That's my job, ma'am. Glad I could be of help."

Pastor Bennett helped Mildred step up onto the front seat of the covered wagon while their three daughters hopped up onto the back of the wagon. The preacher climbed on the front seat, grabbed the reins, and clucked his tongue; the well-trained horses responded immediately, tugging the family and their possessions out of town.

From the swinging doors of the saloon, the three thugs watched the wagon heading northeastward. "We'll give them a little head start and let them get a ways out of town," Tom Crafton, their leader said, as he spat tobacco juice on the floor. "Then we'll pay the girls another visit out along the open road, where no sheriff will be around to protect them."

AS THE BENNETTS EXITED TOWN toward the northeast, the Justice Riders rode into Eureka from the southwest. They tied up their horses at the same supply store where the

Bennetts had been just a few minutes previously. "What do you say we go have a drink before we head on to St. Louis," said Carlos.

"Yeah, my throat is parched. Good idea," agreed Roberto.

"I say you all go get your drink while I get the supplies," Ezra said.

"I'll help you, Ezra," Nate said.

"I may as well join you," Reginald Bonesteel said to Ezra while Harry Whitecloud nodded. "You might need an extra hand." Reginald looked at Carlos and Roberto. "Besides, you boys somehow attract trouble whenever you go into a saloon."

"Reginald has a good point," Ezra said. "Go get your drink, but no trouble this time."

"There will be no trouble, Captain. I promise," said Carlos. "And as for you, Mr. Bonesteel, I'll have you know that we do not get into trouble in *every* saloon we go to. Right, Roberto?"

"Absolutely not!" said Roberto with a mischievous grin, as the twins headed their horses toward the saloon.

The Hawkins twins rode up to the only saloon in town, got off their horses, and hustled inside. They walked up to the bar and ordered two beers. The three hooligans who had harassed the Bennett sisters were still in the saloon, sitting at a table finishing their drinks, preparing to leave and catch up to the Bennetts.

Tom Crafton noticed the twins at the bar sipping their beers. "Hey, Joe, this rot-gut whiskey has me seeing double!" Tom called out to the bartender. "How about it, boys?"

"Yeah, we're seeing double, too," Tom's friends chortled.

Carlos and Roberto turned and glanced at the loudmouths and then returned to sipping their beer, choosing to ignore them.

But Tom Crafton was relentless. "Hey, Jeb," he said loudly to one of the other guys, "which one of those fellows do you think is real?"

"Maybe neither one is real," Jeb drawled. "Maybe they're a mirage."

"Hey, you! You, over there," Tom called in the direction of the Hawkins twins. "Are we seeing double, or are you a mirage?" The men in the bar burst into laughter.

Carlos calmly replied, "We are what is known as identical twins, so you are not seeing double, and we are not a mirage."

The three thugs finished their drinks, got up, and walked over to the twins. "I have to see for myself," said Tom. He grabbed Carlos's cheeks and squeezed. "Yep, he's real."

Carlos started to react with his deadly left hook, but Roberto said, "Remember, brother, no trouble."

Then Tom squeezed Roberto's cheeks. "Yep, he's real, too." Roberto clenched his fists, ready to throw his deadly right hook, but Carlos said, "Huh, uh, uhh, Roberto, no trouble."

Tom Crafton and his cohorts laughed and walked out of the saloon, leaving Carlos and Roberto standing at the bar, steaming. The twins guzzled the dregs of their beers and stormed out of the saloon.

Ezra and the others rode up just as the twins stepped off the boardwalk. The twins grabbed their horses' reins and leaped into their saddles, still steaming.

"I'm glad to see that beer cooled you boys off," said Nate, chuckling.

"Yes, what are you two so riled about?" asked Reginald Bonesteel.

The twins answered at the same time. "Nothing!" they snorted as they turned their horses and rode out of town in the same direction as the Bennetts.

THE BENNETTS' COVERED WAGON bounced over the pockmarked trail. The girls sat in the back, looking out the open end of the wagon, when Sara spotted something odd in the distance. "Papa, there are three men on horseback up on the hill, looking at us," Sara said.

"Are they the three that were in town?" asked Pastor Bennett.

"I can't tell; they are too far away."

"What if they are the same men?" cried Ruth. "They may want to try to kiss us again," she said as she started crying.

"Stop crying, Ruth," said Mary. "It's probably not even them."

"If they start riding toward us, let me know, girls," said Pastor Bennett.

"OK, Papa," said Mary.

The Bennett wagon rounded a turn in the trail, and the girls watched as the three men disappeared over the hill.

"They rode off, Papa," declared Mary. "See, Ruth. I told you there was nothing to worry about."

"Why don't we sing 'Amazing Grace'?" suggested Mildred. "It will help refresh our spirits."

Mrs. Bennett began singing, "Amazing grace, how sweet the sound," and everyone joined in, even Pastor Bennett. As they were singing, the wagon eased around another bend. Just then a rope flew around Pastor Bennett's shoulders, tightening on him and jerking him out of the wagon. "Octavius!" Mildred shrieked.

The girls in the back of the wagon screamed even louder as they saw the two dirty, unshaven men riding up behind the wagon. The third man had hidden behind a rock formation and lassoed the pastor as the wagon was passing by.

"Hello there, little honeys," Tom Crafton said deviously. "Ain't you girls gonna introduce us to your mama and papa?"

THE JUSTICE RIDERS were riding along at a comfortable pace, so Bonesteel said to the Hawkins twins, "Are you still not going to tell us what got you so riled up back there in town?"

"No way," Carlos said. "I'm just now starting to calm down."

"Besides, it's embarrassing," said Roberto.

"Now we all want to know!" said Nate.

A loud popping sound rang out in the distance, bringing an abrupt end to the Justice Riders' banter.

"Gunfire, Captain!" Bonesteel shouted.

"Let's find out what it's all about!" Ezra answered. The Justice Riders spurred their horses and galloped in the direction of the shot. Rounding the bend, they saw a covered wagon stopped in the middle of the trail. Two men were wrestling to hold four women, while another man was beating the tar out of a man who definitely didn't know how to fight or wouldn't.

The Justice Riders charged in with guns drawn, just as Tom Crafton threw a smashing right-handed blow into Pastor Bennett's face, dropping him to the ground.

"That's enough!" Ezra shouted at Tom Crafton, pointing his gun at Crafton's chest. Tom Crafton backed away from the pastor toward his two buddies.

"Let the women go," Harry Whitecloud commanded the two men who were holding the Bennett girls and their mother. Something about the way the tall, strong Indian spoke caused the two thugs to unhand the women.

Ezra dropped off his horse next to the man who had taken the beating. "Are you OK?" he asked as he knelt down next to him.

The man nodded as his wife ran over to wipe the blood from his face.

Ruth, the youngest daughter, cried out, "Mama, they killed our milk cow!"

Nathaniel York rose up to his full stature with seething indignation. "Why would you shoot this family's cow?" Nate asked angrily.

"This has nothing to do with you," Crafton retorted, "so why don't you just go on your way?"

Carlos said, "Oh, but you are so wrong. This has *everything* to do with us." He turned toward Bonesteel and said, "You all wanted to know what got us so riled in the saloon? These three bums are what got us so *riled* up. Captain, will you take that 'no trouble' sign off us now?"

"It's off," Ezra nodded, glaring at the three men, realizing that the scum deserved a lesson.

Carlos and Roberto got off their horses and walked toward the three. Roberto said, "Let me."

"No, I'm the oldest."

"Yeah, by thirty seconds!"

Carlos walked up to Crafton, squeezed his cheeks hard and shoved him to the ground. "Does that feel real to you?" he glowered.

"Yeah, that's real," Crafton said, spitting the dirt out of his mouth. "Now you're going to feel my real fists," he said, scrambling to his feet. "Let's see how soft those cute cheeks of yours really are."

"I was hoping you'd say something like that," Carlos growled.

"I can't stand all this sweet talk," Roberto said sarcastically, as he hauled off and punched Jeb, one of the men with Crafton. The other man, still standing, took a cut at Roberto, but Roberto ducked and caught him with a short left to the ribs and an uppercut to the chin. The man dropped like a rock.

Carlos hit Crafton with two more crushing blows, sending him to the ground again. All three of the Eureka thugs were sprawled on the ground as Ezra said, "Alright, that's enough. They have a long walk ahead of them."

Tom Crafton slowly got up from the ground. "What do you mean, 'walk'?"

"I figure that your three horses will compensate this family for the loss of their cow," Ezra replied.

"You can't do that!" Crafton protested.

Ezra walked over to Crafton and looked him right in the eyes. "I haven't finished yet," he said. "Now take off your boots and give us your guns."

As Tom Crafton stared into Ezra's eyes, he realized, *Those twin boys are tough, but this man is deadly.* Crafton slowly dropped to the ground and started removing his boots; the other two ruffians followed suit while Carlos and Roberto went over and grabbed their guns.

"Maybe you'll have a Damascus Road experience as you are walking back to town," Nate said.

"What?"

"Just like the man named Saul who realized that he'd been working against God and needed to turn around and mend his ways, maybe you boys will have some sort of divine revelation, too," Nate said.

"What are you talking about?" Crafton snarled.

Nate shrugged. "Then again, maybe not."

The three men began walking gingerly down the road, back toward Eureka.

HARRY WHITECLOUD NOTICED Mildred Bennett patching up her husband, so the strong but compassionate Indian went over to offer his assistance. "Let's check to make sure there are no broken bones," he said to her as he knelt down and began gently squeezing Pastor Bennett's arms and legs and running his fingertips over the pastor's rib cage.

"Are you a doctor?" Mildred asked, looking up at Harry hopefully.

"One day I will be."

THE BENNETT GIRLS were gazing starry-eyed at Roberto and Carlos and thanking them over and over again for teaching the villains a lesson.

"Yeah, they tried to kiss us in town," Ruth squealed.

"Ruth! That's enough," said her oldest sister, Mary.

"Well, they did!"

"Well, that's understandable," Carlos said. "After all, you are three beautiful young ladies."

"Oh, do you really think so?" Sara asked, cocking her head slightly sideways.

"Absolutely," Roberto said.

All three girls blushed simultaneously.

"There you go, good as new," Harry Whitecloud said, as he completed bandaging a gash on Pastor Bennett's upper left cheek. "Fortunately, there are no broken bones, so you should be fine in a few days."

"Thank you for your help, friend," Pastor Bennett said. He reached out a hand and firmly shook Harry's hand. The pastor looked at Ezra and the other Justice Riders. "I'm Pastor Joseph Octavius Bennett, and this is my wife Mildred. These are our three daughters, Mary, Ruth, and Sara."

"I'm Ezra Justice, and these are my friends, Nathaniel York, Reginald Bonesteel, and Harry Whitecloud." The Justice Riders stepped forward and shook hands with Pastor and Mrs. Bennett.

"And our two Casanovas over there are Carlos and Roberto Hawkins. Where are you folks headed?"

"We're going to St. Louis to open a church there," replied Pastor Bennett. "I've been reassigned from the Chicago area."

"We're heading to St. Louis ourselves," Ezra said, "and we'd be happy to accompany you."

Pastor Bennett gazed at the girls, who were talking animatedly with Carlos and Roberto; he then looked toward Mildred. "I don't think our girls would mind," he said with a smile.

"No, they certainly wouldn't," she said. They all broke out in a laugh.

"You can accompany us on one condition," Mildred said, looking around at Ezra and his men.

"Yes, ma'am, what might that be?" Ezra asked.

"That I get to cook for you on the way," Mildred answered.

"Ma'am, you don't have to do that," Nate said.

"It would be my pleasure, Mr. York."

"Nate, don't say another word," Reginald Bonesteel said. "I haven't had a home-cooked meal since I don't know when!"

"Well, it's settled then," Mildred said with a smile.

"It's getting late," Ezra said. "Why don't we camp here for the night? You folks have had quite a day, and I'm sure you could use a good night's rest. We'll get an early start tomorrow morning."

"Good idea, Mr. Justice," Pastor Bennett said. "I'm a little whipped . . . literally!" He chuckled at his own joke then winced.

"Carlos and Roberto!" Justice called to the twins. "Can you two tear yourselves away from the young ladies long enough to go butcher the cow?"

"Yeah, oh, eh, yes, sir, Captain!" Roberto called. He and his brother went to their saddles to get their knives.

Later that evening, after the group had finished eating, Reginald Bonesteel commented, "Mrs. Bennett, I can't tell you the last time when I've enjoyed such a delicious meal as you presented this evening."

"Thank you, Mr. Bonesteel. I hope when we get to St. Louis, I can cook you all a meal in a real kitchen!"

"My mouth is watering already," Reginald replied as everyone chuckled.

Nate and Pastor Bennett sat around the campfire, discussing their backgrounds. Nate told Pastor Bennett how he had grown up with Ezra Justice on the Justice family's plantation. "I've always had an appreciation for preachers," Nate said. "My father was our spiritual leader on the plantation." Nate took a sip of coffee, looked into the campfire, and paused as though he was seeing his father in his mind.

He looked up at Pastor Bennett. "Daddy could really preach. "Ezra often came and listened to our services, and he would ask me questions about Jesus all the time. I told him about how Jesus died for our sins and that our lives on this earth are just a blink of an eye. We need to get right with the Lord if we want to have eternal life in heaven."

"How did Mr. Justice respond to that message?" Pastor Bennett asked.

"Ezra is a very analytical man," Nate said, "and he was that way even as a youngster. At that time, what he couldn't see he couldn't believe. Then one night in our service, Ezra was sitting next to me, listening as my father gave a sermon of all sermons. I looked at Ezra and asked what he thought about the message, but he didn't answer. He had the strangest look in his eyes. My dad asked anyone who wanted to know the Lord to come forward. All of a sudden, Ezra stood up and walked to the front to accept Jesus as his Savior.

"I said, 'Thank you, Lord! Ezra was a good man; you just made him a great man!' After the service, I asked Ezra what prompted him to go forward, and Ezra replied, 'He told me to.'"

"I asked him, 'Do you mean that Jesus told you to go up front?' and Ezra said, 'He didn't tell me his name; he just said do it!'"

"Whew!" said Pastor Bennett, "we all pray that the Lord will speak to us, don't we?"

"We sure do, Pastor."

"Well, it seems that he answered your prayers on behalf of Mr. Justice."

Nate glanced over toward Justice. "Yes, sir. Sure nuff does. What about you, Pastor Bennett? What prompts your move to St. Louis?"

"I'm ready for a new challenge. We had a comfortable, secure position in Chicago," Pastor Bennett said, "but we all felt that we wanted to go where we could minister to people of various racial backgrounds. Now that the war is over, a lot of Negroes have been displaced in the St. Louis area, many coming up the Mississippi and staying there along the river. Besides that, there is a large Indian population around St. Louis. Our dream is to have a church where everyone is welcome, regardless of skin color—black, white, red, and every shade in between." Pastor Bennett looked into Nate's face and recognized instinctively that Nate understood the challenges involved with developing such a congregation.

"You must like to ruffle feathers," Nate said with a smile.

"So did Jesus, I think," Pastor Bennett said.

Meanwhile Ezra, Harry, and Reginald had laid out their bed rolls about twenty yards from camp, putting some distance between their locations to give the Bennetts some privacy. Carlos and Roberto were still talking to the Bennett daughters.

Mrs. Bennett called over to the girls, "It's time to get ready for bed, girls. We'll be leaving early in the morning."

"Yes, Mama," Mary called. "We'll be right there."

"Hey, Casanovas," Bonesteel called. "That goes for you also."

"Give us a break. We're just being friendly," Roberto said.

"It's nice to talk to someone sweet for a change," Carlos added.

"I'm sure it is." Bonesteel rolled his eyes. "I'm sure it is."

EARLY THE NEXT MORNING, after the group finished breakfast and broke camp, they packed to continue their journey. The girls now had horses of their own to ride, and they couldn't wait to get started. Two days later they finally arrived in St. Louis.

The Bennetts were met by a committee from their new church congregation and taken to their new home. The Justice Riders accompanied the Bennetts and helped unload their belongings from the wagon.

"We're going to go check in at a hotel now," Ezra told the Bennetts after the last crate had been carried into the house. "And we'll be taking the train to Washington tomorrow."

"Please, Captain Justice. Stay with us tonight," Pastor Bennett offered. "We have plenty of space, and you won't be any bother at all."

"I appreciate that, Pastor Bennett," Ezra said, "but we will be just fine at the hotel."

"Well, then, you must at least take time this evening for a home-cooked meal in my new kitchen," Mrs. Bennett said.

"We definitely have time for that, Mrs. Bennett," Reginald Bonesteel said. "Right, Captain?"

"Wouldn't miss it," Ezra said.

The following morning Pastor Bennett and his family went to the train station to see off the Justice Riders and to thank them again for saving them from the three villains who had attacked them.

Carlos and Roberto walked their horses toward the train to put the animals in the boxcar. Ezra, Nate, and Harry had already tethered their horses in the same boxcar. Mary walked next to Carlos while Sara and Ruth walked with Roberto.

Carlos and Roberto led the horses up the ramp to secure them in the boxcar. "Wait at the bottom of the ramp," Carlos instructed the girls. "The horses can be temperamental sometimes when they are being put in a closed location like this."

"The pastor and I want to thank you for what you have done for us," Mrs. Bennett said to Ezra.

"If you ever get back to St. Louis, please come visit our church," Pastor Bennett added.

"You can count on it, Pastor Bennett," Ezra said.

"I enjoyed our conversation," Nate said, "and I will look forward to hearing one of your sermons."

"And thank you, ma'am, for one of the finest dinners I have ever had in my entire life," said Reginald Bonesteel.

Ezra, Nate, and Bonesteel shook hands with the Bennetts, then turned and walked toward the train to board.

WITH THE HORSES TIED SECURELY in the boxcar, Carlos and Roberto walked back to the Bennett girls.

"Roberto, we're going to miss you!" Sara and Ruth said practically in unison.

"And I'm going to miss you, too, girls," Roberto said with a smile. "You better get back to your parents now. It's about time for us to board our train." Ruth and Sara reluctantly walked back toward their parents, calling out, "Good-bye, Roberto!" about a dozen times as they went.

Roberto waved, turned, and entered one of the train's passenger cars.

Carlos and Mary stood in front of each other awkwardly, not sure what to say. Mary looked down at the ground. "Do you really have to go?" Mary asked Carlos quietly.

"Yes, Mary, I do. We have orders and have to get to Washington right away. But I will be back," he said.

Mary continued looking down toward the ground, knowing that if she looked Carlos in the eyes she might cry. "Well, until you get back . . ." Mary quickly reached up and gave Carlos a quick peck on the cheek. She turned and rushed off.

The Justice Riders settled in for the long, arduous cross-country trip aboard the passenger train. "We might as well get as comfortable as possible," Bonesteel said.

"Easy for you to say," said Harry Whitecloud, as he tried to stretch his long legs under the seat in front of him.

"Get some sleep if you can," Ezra advised. "Next stop, Washington, D.C."

It was raining in Washington as the Justice Riders made their way into town. The streets of the city had turned to mud, but the grand vision of the Capitol inspired the men nonetheless. They tied up their horses in front of the main entrance and trudged up the hill toward the front door.

Once inside, they could hardly contain their awe. "Wow! Look at that!" Roberto said nearly every thirty seconds.

Ezra Justice had been to the U.S. Capitol before, but he was still inspired by the sight. Harry Whitecloud was fascinated by the huge painting of *The Baptism of Pocahontas,* one of the eight paintings depicting historical highlights of the young nation. A surprising number of Indians were included in the Capitol's paintings and sculptures, although they were almost always depicted in some subservient manner. Only the carving of William Penn—founder of Philadelphia, "the City of Brotherly Love"—included an Indian where the white man and the red man stood on equal ground and were of equal height.

Reginald Bonesteel seemed duly impressed with the understated opulence of the Capitol. While most of America's population still lived in log cabins, the imported marble of the Capitol building's interior was especially striking to Ezra and his men as they walked inside the rotunda and headed toward the long corridor where the War Department was temporarily located.

The Capitol's rotunda, reminiscent of an ancient Roman temple, was still under construction when Justice and his men walked through it. This symbol of freedom was being built, as was most of the construction work done on the Capitol, by slave labor. Only the boldest of advocates for emancipation of the slaves dared to mention that the huge blocks of granite, marble, limestone, and other building materials used in the Capitol building were lugged into place through the back-breaking labor of slaves and immigrants. After all, many of the nation's founding fathers—men such as George Washington and Thomas Jefferson—had owned substantial numbers of black slaves.

Since 1820, slavery had been the major issue that dominated the speeches on Capitol Hill, in both branches of Congress—the Senate and the House of Representatives. Powerful orators such as Daniel Webster, John C. Calhoun, and Henry Clay—the man who passionately tried and failed to reconcile the interests of the North and the South before the war—argued the merits or plagues of slavery, with the Dred Scott decision being passed down by the Supreme Court in 1857, declaring that Negroes were not citizens of the United States. It remained to be seen, now that the war was over, if anything would really change within these hallowed halls.

A young-looking lieutenant, sharply dressed in a clean Federal Army uniform with polished brass and boots, met the Justice Riders at the door of the War Department's temporary office. "Come in, gentlemen. Sit down, please." He motioned toward several chairs spaced around the room.

"Thank you, Lieutenant," Ezra replied. He and Nate moved toward the chairs. Carlos and Roberto continued to stand just inside the doorway, gazing at the beautifully appointed, long, narrow room with high, ornately decorated ceilings. Harry Whitecloud stepped over to the fireplace mantle where he found an old French sword to admire. Bonesteel seemed more enamored of the fantastic view looking out the tall, narrow windows on the front of the Capitol building.

"General Sherman will be with you momentarily," the lieutenant said. "He is greatly anticipating your meeting. Would you care for something to drink while you wait? Bourbon, brandy, coffee?"

"No, thank you, Lieutenant," Ezra said. "We'll just sit here and wait until the general is ready for us."

"As you wish, sir."

General Sherman's unmistakable, gruff voice could be heard in the side anteroom, barking out commands to his office staff. A moment later he appeared in the receiving room where the Justice Riders were waiting for him. Dressed in rumpled military blues, his scruffy beard unkempt as usual, he looked only slightly less disheveled than when he'd been camped on the outskirts of Atlanta less than a year previously.

Sherman's eyes twinkled, nonetheless, like those of a man who had been relieved of a huge burden on his back.

"Captain Justice!" he bellowed as Ezra and his men jumped up and saluted the general. Sherman touched his right forefinger to his forehead, casually returning their salute, as he strode across the room and clasped Ezra's hand. "So good to see you again."

"Hello, General. It's good to see you as well."

"I'm glad you're safe, Justice. I thought that we might lose you several times over this past year: all that nasty stuff with those renegades led by Mordecai Slate, and then there was that horrible incident with the *Sultana*. You and your men are to be commended for your bravery and your willingness to risk your own lives to help save your fellow soldiers and the civilians aboard that fateful vessel."

"Thank you, sir. It was a night none of us will ever forget."

"Sit down. Please, have a seat." Sherman waved the men back to their seats and pulled up a chair next to Ezra Justice. "I'm still getting used to all this office work around here. I never dreamed what all it took to run an army. I liked things a lot better when General Grant was running the show and I was a general out in the field, on the front lines, rather than working indoors so much of the time. Now that I'm in charge of the army, I spend half my time *talking* about reconstruction matters and the other half *talking* about Indian issues. I'm not cut out for this desk life. I'm a fighter."

"Yes, sir, I know that," Ezra replied.

"Well, no doubt, you men are wondering why I sent for you."

"That did cross our minds, General," Ezra said with a slight smile.

"Well, first of all, I want to congratulate you on a job well done. Outstanding, nothing short of outstanding. The way you men tore up those supply trains and sabotaged enemy movements, demoralizing the Confederate troops with your unusual attacks, you probably helped us end the war a good year or two earlier than we might have otherwise. For that, I am grateful, as are the American people, and . . ." Sherman paused, "so is the President of the United States."

"The President?"

"That's correct. I told the President that the war would still be going on if it hadn't been for your efforts in the South. President Andrew Johnson is impressed with you men, especially with you, Captain Justice. The President wants to bestow on you the Congressional Medal of Honor, our country's highest honor for a military man. Congratulations, Justice."

General Sherman reached across the arms of the chair and shook Justice's hand again. "We'll have a formal ceremony with the President while you are here, but I wanted to tell you about this honor myself and to have the privilege of congratulating you in person."

"Congratulations, indeed," Reginald Bonesteel said, standing and stepping across to shake Ezra's hand.

"It has been an honor to serve with you, Captain," Harry Whitecloud said, following behind Bonesteel.

"Way to go, Cap'n!" Carlos hooted.

"Nobody deserves such an honor more than you, Captain," Roberto said.

Nathaniel York was next, and despite being in the nation's Capitol with the army's commanding officer, he could not restrain his emotions. Tears welled in his eyes. He and Ezra had been friends since childhood—more than friends really, almost like brothers, despite the fact that Nate had grown up as a slave on the Justice family plantation. But Ezra Justice and his family had never treated Nate as anything but an equal, an employee who helped make the plantation a home and successful family business. Nate had served in the Tennessee Colored Battery under General George H. Thomas before signing on with Ezra Justice's elite squad. Together, he and Ezra had survived numerous near-death experiences, and Nate had watched Ezra slowly but surely trust God with his life. It was a transformation that Nate had prayed for since both he and Ezra were boys. Now, his friend—his brother—was to be honored by the President of the United States.

Large tears formed and dropped from Nate's eyes as he held onto Ezra's shoulders and spoke quietly: "The Good Book says to humble yourself under the mighty hand of God, and he will exalt you at the proper time. You've been faithful to him, Ezra, and now God is rewarding you with this honor. It ain't nothin' compared to what you'll have up in heaven, but it is a nice reminder that when you do the right thing, God notices."

"Thank you, Nate," Ezra said. "That means a lot to me— from all of you."

Ezra fell quiet and bowed his head, looking at the floor in a long, awkward silence. He took a deep breath and then looked back at Sherman. "I'm honored, General, that you and the President want to present this medal to me, but I can't accept it."

"What?" Sherman nearly choked on the pipe he had been lighting while the other men congratulated Ezra. "What are you talking about, Justice? This is the highest honor bestowed by the President of the United States. What do you mean, you can't accept it. Of course you can! Of course, you *will*."

"I understand that, sir," said Justice, "and I appreciate you and the President thinking that I deserve this medal. But if the medal is to be given out, there is one man on our team who deserves it much more than I do—and that is Sergeant Shaun O'Banyon. You may recall that I wired you to inform you that O'Banyon sacrificed his life to save us and a platoon of Union soldiers."

"Yes, yes, I do recall that," Sherman said between puffs on his pipe.

Nathaniel York sat down in his chair and put his elbows on his knees, his arms and hands supporting his head as he let out a low whisper, "Oh, yes, I see it now, Captain. The Bible says, 'Greater love hath no man than he lay down his life for a friend,' and we all know that is exactly what O'Banyon did for us. If it hadn't been for O'Banyon, we would never have been able to take care of Slate's gang; and we wouldn't have been aboard the *Sultana* when the boat caught fire. We couldn't have saved anyone if Shaun hadn't first saved us . . ." Nate's voice trailed off, and he closed his eyes, almost as if praying.

"That's exactly right, Nate," Ezra said. He turned back to General Sherman. "So I would greatly appreciate it, General, if you could convince the President to award the medal to Sergeant Shaun O'Banyon."

Sherman remained silent, puffing his pipe, sending large curls of smoke floating toward the high ceiling. He rubbed his chin as he stared at Ezra Justice, then looked from man to man, each of the Justice Riders looking right into the eyes of the general.

He turned his gaze back to Justice. "This is highly irregular, Captain Justice."

"Irregular or not, the men and I here just did our duty as good soldiers. Sergeant O'Banyon went beyond the call of duty."

"Mmm-hmm." Sherman blew more smoke around his head.

"O'Banyon is the real hero, General."

"Alright, alright! I get it, Captain," Sherman boomed. "Let me see what I can do. I'll try to convince the President to award the Congressional Medal of Honor to Sergeant Shaun O'Banyon, although I think you are nuts." Sherman shook his head as he leaned back in his chair, puffing on his pipe.

"Thank you, General," Ezra said. "For the medal part . . ."

The men in the room burst into laughter; even cagey old General Sherman let out a good belly laugh.

"Well, good. Now I want to get around to why I called you and your men here—besides the medal issue, that is." Sherman took a final puff on his pipe before putting it down in a saucer on a table behind him.

"The President has put me in charge of trying to clean up the lawlessness currently running rampant in the midwestern and western parts of our country. We're putting things back together with the South, little by little. It is going to take some time, no question about it. But meanwhile, we've lost control of the situation out west. I need some good lawmen to bring order to the territory."

"What does that have to do with us, General?" Ezra asked.

"I would like for you and your men to become U.S. marshals," Sherman said with a satisfied look on his face. "There's a lot of work to do now that the war is over. You would have freedom to travel wherever you need to go, bringing law and order to bear on the situations as you find them. Sometimes you would be helping local sheriffs, and at other times you'd be the only lawmen in the region for hundreds of miles around. The government would provide you with a decent salary, and you could live anywhere you want, as long as you get the job done. What do you say?"

Ezra Justice nodded his head. He immediately understood the profound ramifications of General Sherman's offer. And after more than four years of war, living in tents and surviving out of a backpack, the call of the wild was not nearly as attractive to him as it might have been prior to the war.

Justice spoke quietly but firmly. "Thanks for the offer, General. But Nate and I are heading home to Tennessee. We want to go home to the plantation where we grew up. My parents are dead, but Nate still has family there. And of course, I still own the land. From what I understand, there were several big battles nearby, so my property may not be recognizable any longer. But we want to go home to see if there is anything we can salvage. Even if things are burned or destroyed, it is still our home. I won't speak for the others, but

I'm going to have to respectfully decline your most generous offer."

Nathaniel York nodded his head. "I'm with Captain Justice, General Sherman. I want to go home."

"I understand, men. I do. What about the rest of you? Any takers?" General Sherman looked at the Hawkins twins as though expecting an answer.

"Roberto and I are going back to St. Louis and from there probably on down to New Orleans," Carlos said. He paused and smiled. "We want to see what sort of trouble we can get into down in N'awlins!"

Roberto elbowed Carlos in the side. "What my brother means, General . . ."

"I know exactly what your brother means, Son. I've been in the army a long time. I don't blame you for wanting to get out and have some fun. Especially after these past few years, fun has become a rarity."

"Yes, sir," Roberto replied, glaring at Carlos. "That's what my brother meant."

"What about you, Sergeant Bonesteel? Interested? Whitecloud? You'd make a good lawman, especially in some of those territories where we are having trouble with the Indians. How about it? Are you going to be my marshals?"

"I'd be delighted to take you up on your offer, General Sherman," Reginald Bonesteel began. Sherman's eyes lit up. "But I am heading for California, where I plan to strike it rich in this country by digging for gold. I must respectfully decline, as well."

General Sherman looked at Whitecloud. "Let me guess. You have postwar plans, too."

"Yes, General, I do," Harry Whitecloud said. "As for me, I'm going to continue my medical studies; and when I become a doctor, I want to return to my people, the Sioux, and help them."

"Six Justice Riders and not a U.S. marshal in the bunch," Sherman said with a slight laugh. "Well, I won't say that I'm not disappointed. I am. But on the other hand I'm not surprised. I certainly understand your desire to get back to some semblance of normalcy after the turmoil we've all experienced in our lives these past four years. But let's do this: let's keep the offer on the table. The President has given me the authority to hire the best U.S. marshals I can find, and as far as I'm concerned, you men are the best. As long as I'm in charge, the offer will always be open for you. If you get out there and you decide that you'd like to take me up on becoming U.S. marshals, just let me know, and the job is yours."

"That's certainly more than fair, General," Ezra said. "We appreciate your confidence in us. Only God knows what the future holds, so we won't rule out the possibility of working together again."

Sherman nodded and reached again for his pipe. "Alright, fine. Let's go back to that seventh Justice Rider, O'Banyon. Now about this Medal of Honor. Since Sergeant O'Banyon is unable to accept the medal, we will have to award it posthumously, but to whom should we give it? Does he have any surviving kin?"

"Yes, he does, General. You can present it to Lizzie . . . er, I mean, Elizabeth O'Banyon, Sergeant O'Banyon's wife," Ezra replied.

"Where's she located?"

"She has a farm a short distance outside of Clinton, Missouri."

"Alright. I'll see that she gets the medal," General Sherman said, as he succeeded in relighting the pipe. "I may even take it to her personally. I'll be down in that part of the country looking for my lawmen, anyway, so it would be good to present the medal to her face-to-face. You know, of course, that not many of these medals are given out."

"Maybe so, General. But the finest medal won't replace her husband," Ezra offered cautiously.

Sherman nodded in understanding. Both he and Justice hated the war they had fought and won. They hated the killing, the destruction of property, the ripping apart of families—the shredding of the whole nation, really. But it had to be done, and the war had to be won, or else there would be two separate countries instead of one known as the United States of America. Sherman lived with his own perpetual sense of grief over the war. He understood pain, and he could tell by the expressions on the faces of the Justice Riders that the death of their companion still nagged at them in the night when nobody else could see their inner tears or hear their silent screams. Sherman knew, better than most.

He stood up abruptly and cleared his throat, signaling that the meeting was over. "Well, good luck to all of you," he said, already beginning to move from man to man, shaking hands. "And remember, that U.S. marshal's job is always open."

"Thanks, General. We'll keep that in mind," Justice replied. "Please express my humble thanks to the President."

"Mmm, yes, the President. I'll have to work on that one. I doubt he's ever had anyone turn down even a relatively minor citation, much less a Congressional Medal of Honor. But for the sake of O'Banyon, I'll risk the President's ire."

"Thank you, again, General. I truly appreciate it," Ezra said. "No doubt if you'd seen Elizabeth O'Banyon handling a gun when she was fighting off Mordecai Slate's bunch, you might want to give her a separate medal for bravery in the line of duty. She's quite a woman."

"I believe that, Justice," General Sherman replied, as the men began moving toward the door. "I'll look forward to meeting her.

"Lieutenant! Please see these men out, and be sure to take care of anything they need while they are here in the city."

"Yes, sir!" the young lieutenant snapped to attention. "This way, gentlemen. It is my pleasure to serve you."

The Justice Riders exited General Sherman's office and walked back through the long corridors of the Capitol building. When they got outside, they noticed that the rain had stopped and the sun had come out. The skies were bright blue. It was like a new day had dawned. And in a way, for each of the Justice Riders, it had. At last they were able to strike out on their own in a united country to seek out the dreams each one of them held inside.

As the men trudged down the hill to retrieve their horses, reality hit them; they were going their separate ways. "Where are you off to?" Bonesteel asked Harry Whitecloud.

"Well, there's a train that will get me as far as Philadelphia, and I can go by horseback the rest of the way back to Princeton," Harry said. "What about you?"

"California," Bonesteel answered immediately. "Or maybe Texas. Or both. But I'd like to try my hand at panning for gold, so California is a good bet for me."

"Let's try to keep in touch," Roberto said, as the men arrived at their horses.

The Justice Riders said quick good-byes and started to mount up. Nobody wanted to prolong the agony of splitting up.

"Remember, let's all keep in contact with Elizabeth O'Banyon," Ezra said. "If any of you need our help, you'll know how to reach us. Just let Elizabeth know, and she can pass the word to the rest of us. All you have to say is, 'Remember O'Banyon,' and we are on our way. May God be with you, men!"

"And with you," each man called back.

"I hope God has been merciful," Nate said, wondering what he and Ezra might find when they returned to the Justice plantation.

The sun was setting near the end of the day as Ezra and Nate rode through a clearing along the line of the river, looking for a defensible campsite close to the water.

The war is over, Ezra mused. *I should start thinking like a civilian.* The two men had been traveling all day long, leaving Washington before dawn by train, going as far as Roanoke, Virginia, and then traveling by horseback down along the Appalachian Mountain range on their way to Tennessee. It was a rigorous trip, and Ezra recognized that the animals were getting as tired as he and Nate. The Appaloosa mare Ezra rode had already stumbled twice.

Ezra's eyes rose to the ridgeline and spotted a small grove of cottonwood trees that looked appealing. Oftentimes good grass could be found near the cottonwoods, and as the shadows lengthened, Ezra decided that was as good a spot as any to bed down for the evening.

Nathaniel York saw the cottonwoods about the same time, and without saying a word, he knew that Ezra had made a decision. They pulled up their horses under the trees, and both men wearily slid down the sides of the strong animals. They unbuckled the mountain straps holding the saddles in place, released the cinch straps, and pulled the saddles off. They dropped their gear in a pile.

Ezra and Nate had traveled together for so many years that they had developed a routine and an economy of words and motion between the two of them. Spoken words often proved unnecessary; sharing the workload came naturally. Neither man had to say, "Please do this," or "Please do that." They were both self-starters who saw a need and filled it.

Nathaniel began systematically rubbing down the horses and picking their hooves clean of any debris. Then, as Ezra gathered fodder for the horses and walked them to the water, Nate snapped dry branches from a nearby cottonwood and began building an "Indian fire," a small, barely discernable campfire, to avoid detection by potential enemies. Ezra realized that few potential enemies were stalking the cottonwoods, but old habits are hard to break.

Nathaniel pulled the small, battered coffeepot from his saddlebags. He sat down cross-legged next to the fire and laid out a small canvas pouch containing an oily rag and his gun-cleaning supplies. Ezra shucked his ten-shot .32 caliber LaMat and his cross-draw .44 caliber Navy Colt and methodically began cleaning the weapons.

Meanwhile, Nate walked back toward his kit, pausing long enough to drop his .44 Colt and his 12-guage shotgun at Ezra's knees. Then Nathaniel dug into the bottom of his leather kit and brought out his favorite mixture of coffee and chicory.

Nate noticed Ezra's caustic glance and said, "Lord a-mercy! You're not going to start in on the coffee again, are you?"

Ezra smiled and continued to wipe down the weapons.

Nathaniel filled the pot with water and shoved it into the coals. He went back to his kit and found two battered tin coffee cups.

As was their habit, the men settled back and allowed their senses to take in their new environment. They listened to the sounds of the water rippling nearby, the soft rustle of the crisp evening breeze. The air was latent with the scent of pine trees mixed with the aroma of the brewing coffee. Both men were accustomed to being perpetually on the alert and instinctively aware of their surroundings, but now that the war was over, they were trying to adjust to becoming men of peace.

Nathaniel had picketed the horses comfortably under a low-hanging bow of a cottonwood tree. As always, the men kept their horses in the line of sight. They both knew there was no better sentry than a horse. At any sign of movement during the night, the horses' heads would come up with their ears pricked and eyes staring in the direction of the trouble.

Nate toed the coffeepot deeper into the embers. "Coffee's ready, Cap'n," Nate said.

Ezra grunted in acknowledgment as Nathaniel passed him a cup. Ezra spun the noxious brew in the container and took a sip. "You know, Nate, in all the years you've been making coffee, this, tonight, is the best you've ever made."

"Ezra, are you getting sentimental in your old age?" They looked at each other and laughed.

The two men had known each other for over forty years; they thought alike and fought alike, but the one area of human existence that divided them was not the fact that Nate's skin was black and Ezra's was white. No, they parted company when it came to the brewing of coffee.

Both men quietly sipped their coffee, looking into the fire in silence. The two of them rarely spoke of the horrors they had survived during the War between the States, but for some reason it seemed appropriate as they got closer to their home. "It will be a comfort to lay our heads on the bedrolls tonight without having to worry about the war," Nate said quietly.

Ezra nodded, "You're right, Nate, but for some men the war will never be over."

"What do you mean?"

"The scars of this conflict were not just physical. Men and women were changed forever. Brother fought against brother. It's going to take some time to pull our country back together. There's a lot of work to do. I read recently in *Harper's Gazette* that six hundred thousand Americans died in this terrible conflict. We have killed our own countrymen during the war, and we've killed others in the name of justice since Appomattox. The country reeks of death."

Nate dropped his head and closed his eyes, thinking of the horrendously bloody scenes they had witnessed together.

Justice was still talking. "I've been thinking a lot about where our country is headed, Nate. Most people don't realize that America is at a crossroads. There's a vast western continent that is yet to be settled and explored. How we handle that and the way we parcel out that land will make or break us. I pray that the terrible price we paid for freedom will pay off for our countrymen."

Ezra paused then said, "Nate, I've been wanting to tell you something."

"Sure thing, Captain. What is it?"

"Do you know that hundred acres north of the big stand of Ponderosa pine trees?"

"Sure I do. That's some of the best-producing land on the entire plantation."

"Well, I've wired the county courthouse and told them that the parcel now belongs to you."

"I don't understand," Nate gasped. "Are you saying . . . ?"

"That's right; that's exactly what I'm saying. Your people have worked that land for as far back as anyone can remember. It's only right that it should belong to you. Now it's yours under the law."

"Ezra, I can't let you do that!"

"There's nothing more to be said. It's already done."

Nate took a deep breath. He knew better than to argue with Ezra Justice. "Ezra, I'll be indebted to you forever."

"Let's get some sleep, neighbor."

Nate liked the sound of that term. *Neighbor.* He took a long sip of coffee and swirled it in his mouth. "You're right, Ezra. Tonight, this coffee is especially good."

THE MORNING SUN had barely peeked over the horizon when Ezra opened his eyes; he remained motionless and silent, listening for danger. His senses took in the sights and sounds around him, quickly scanning the immediate area. He glanced at the horses and was reassured when he noticed the animals grazing idly. Ezra shook his head. *How long is it going to take me to get over this paranoia, always looking for an enemy out there?* he wondered. *The war is over, Ezra; get over it.*

Looking to his right, Ezra was surprised to discover Nate still fast asleep. Nate's face was one of peace and tranquility. Ezra envied Nathaniel's childlike faith in God that provided such an ability to sleep so soundly. Nate possessed a confidence that went far beyond his own strength.

"Nathaniel," Ezra said gently. Nate didn't budge.

"Nathaniel York, it's time that we got moving."

"Huh, oh—oh, sorry, Cap'n, I was dreamin' of the plantation. It's been a long time since I've been back there. I sure hope I'm up to runnin' my own place." Nate bounded to his feet and brushed the dust from his clothing.

"You'll do a fine job, Nate. It's well-known that your grandfather was a hard worker when he accompanied Lewis and Clark on their exploration of the Northwest Territories. Your parents were hard workers, too, on the plantation in Tennessee, and they raised you to be the same."

Nathaniel smiled as he thought about his grandfather. It was a source of family pride that Grandpa York had been instrumental in the success of the famous Lewis and Clark expedition of 1803. He became one of the best-known black men in America at the time, and the public respect afforded him—although he remained a slave for years—contributed greatly to Nathaniel's quiet self-confidence.

"We can't get there if we don't get going." Ezra's voice punctured Nate's reverie.

"You're right, Cap'n," Nate replied. "I'm ready to get started on a whole new way of living." Nate turned his boots upside down and shook them violently to make certain no unexpected guests had taken up residence during the night. The men saddled their horses and pointed them toward the southwest, toward home.

FOR TWO DAYS THE HAWKINS TWINS and Reginald Bonesteel had been doing nothing but enjoying the luxuries of Washington—which to them meant the company of fine ladies and fine liquor—all compliments of General Sherman. But now it was time to get on with their quest.

"Come on, Reginald; don't be so stubborn," Carlos Hawkins said, as Bonesteel and the twins sat in their Washington hotel dining room having dinner. Harry Whitecloud had already caught the train to Philadelphia, and Ezra and Nate had left for the plantation.

"Stubborn? Me? Surely you must be speaking of someone else," Reginald Bonesteel replied.

"Then why don't you travel with us to St. Louis, and we can continue the party there?" Roberto added.

"Sure, let's travel together. It will be fun," Carlos said as he slapped Bonesteel on the back.

"Fun? Me? Traveling with you?"

"Oh, come on, you old toad. Live a little," Carlos said with a smile. "What are you worried about? We've been showing you the real world for the last two days."

"I know! You nearly killed me."

"We'll take good care of you, Reginald," Roberto quipped. "As you have found out, when you are with the handsome Hawkins twins, it is a lot easier to meet the ladies."

"I've done quite well on my own, thank you," Bonesteel sniffed.

"We would have never known it these past two days," Carlos said, laughing.

"Seriously, Reginald. We've had a great time with you," Roberto said. "We're not going to interfere with your plans, but since you're going to California, why not travel with us to St. Louis and then continue on to California from there?"

"Well, I guess I could do that. And it would be almost like having someone to talk to along the way," Bonesteel said.

"Almost?" Carlos said, raising his eyebrows. "I can't believe you want to wander around, digging in mud, when you could be dancing with beautiful women and, more importantly, enjoying our fine company." Carlos frowned, pretending that his feelings were hurt.

"Oh, alright. I'll wipe your noses to St. Louis. But I'm only going to stay a couple of days, then I'm heading to California to make my fortune. I want to get through Memphis before the rough weather sets in," Bonesteel said.

"Oh, Reginald, after a couple of days partying with the Hawkins twins in St. Louis, you'll have second thoughts about going to California," Roberto said.

"Maybe so, Roberto," Bonesteel said, smiling. "Let's get there and see what happens."

Exuding power and command, Stanton R. Black, a former Confederate Brigadier General, stood at the front of a dimly lit law office in Pulaski, Tennessee, where nearly thirty men were crowded into the front foyer. They had come to hear about Black's new organization, part of the Ku Klux Klan, which Black and his friends had originally started as a joke. In the immediate aftermath of the war, as the fall of 1865 turned into the early winter of 1866, Black and some fellow Confederate veterans formed a small group of rebels who took great pleasure in marching through their hometowns covered in white sheets, trying to frighten the recently freed slaves, pretending that the sheeted creatures where ghosts of slain Confederate soldiers.

They named their group after a Greek word, *kuklos,* meaning a circle, implying an inner circle of friends, a club. By May 1866, the group had grown larger and more organized, comprised mostly of former members of the Confederate Army.

The idea of a "Klan," purposely misspelled, was another joke added later. Even the weird names of the group's officers—Imperial Wizard, Grand Turk, Grand Cyclops, and others—were intended initially as colossal jokes. But the fledgling Ku Klux Klan was no longer a joking matter. With Black stirring the pot of racial hatred, things had turned violent early on as disgruntled southerners found the Klan a convenient means of keeping black people "in their place." Already the Klan had established a reputation for terror and death. In Black's demented mind, there was no gray area. Any person who supported the advancement of Negroes—whether politically, socially, or educationally—was an enemy.

Before long, branches of the Klan were springing up all over the South. One of the early Grand Wizards was Nathan Bedford Forrest, the wily Confederate cavalry commander whom Ezra Justice and his men had tricked into thinking that a large Union Army lay between his location outside Spring Hill, Tennessee, and the town of Franklin. No doubt, had Forrest's forty-five hundred mounted troops arrived earlier in Franklin, General John M. Schofield's Union Army might not have been able to slip away in the middle of the night. And the battle of Franklin might have produced a much different result.

Now, even though the war was over, Nathan Forrest continued his own crusade against the former slaves. He enlisted white men, and some white women as well, from every profession and class, including a number of southern lawmen. Sadly, even some misguided members of the clergy joined the Klan's efforts to maintain white supremacy over the black population in the South.

Wearing white sheets over their clothing, masks over their faces, and pointed white cardboard hats (later replaced by cloth caps), the Klan executed most of its raids at night. They broke into the homes of black families, dragging them from their beds, women and children included, usually burning the home to the ground. They tortured the former slaves in some of the most inhumane ways imaginable, and often killed the black people, as well as any white sympathizers. Although no one could have imagined it at the time, that made the return of Ezra Justice and Nathaniel York a threat to the Klan . . . and the Klan a threat to Justice.

STANTON R. BLACK silenced the room and launched into his recruitment speech. "Good men of the South." He paused, noticing that several women had joined the crowd, as well. "And noble women, I might add.

"Since the Federal Army started imposing its laws on our land, many of us have witnessed decent white people being harassed on our sidewalks by gangs of loose Negroes full of arrogance and carrying weapons. We cannot allow our women and children to be terrorized by these renegades! We must act now to protect our pure race and prevent further rebellion on the part of these darkies."

"Here, here! That's right!" a man in a dark suit called out.

Stanton nodded approvingly toward the man before continuing his diatribe. "Therefore, along with certain high officials and respectable leaders here in Tennessee, I have called this meeting tonight for the purpose of further organizing our efforts to maintain order in Pulaski and any nearby town where this sort of rebellion from Negroes exists. Furthermore, we cannot allow scalawags and carpetbaggers sympathetic to the radical Republican Party in Congress and the like to intimidate us with their professed Reconstruction Acts and Ironclad Oaths. Their Freedmen's Bureau established by the U.S. Congress fully intends to pit the darkies against us, providing money to open schools and hospitals, as well as houses and food, for our former slaves. We must stand together to resist this so-called reconstruction, for it will be the ruin of the South if we allow the government to encourage insolence among the black race.

"Our God didn't intend for darkies to be educated or to have social privileges. The good reverend over there teaches us that." Black pointed to Reverend Jason Jackson, minister at one of the larger churches in Pulaski. Reverend Jackson took a step forward and raised his hand, letting the others in the crowd know that he was in agreement with Black's assessment.

"Besides, slavery is for the good of this province. Our crops cannot be left to rot and our fields untended because of unruly slaves. White men of the South must remember our indisputable rights and work against this sedition!"

"You tell 'em, Stanton!" a small man shouted, raising his fist in the air.

"Your acceptance and your declaration to resist the Republican Party, the Freedmen's Bureau, and the Loyal League, or any individuals sympathetic to their cause, qualifies you for membership in the Pulaski, Tennessee, order of the Ku Klux Klan, known hereafter as the Tennessee Realm, supported by prudent men—and women—whose purposes are to be achieved by the disarmament of black renegades and to further prevent their learning, and especially to forbid them from voting, sitting on juries, or testifying against white folk, which will result in undue power and intimidation."

"Lousy fiends, no better 'n fleas!" a female voice sounded from the back of the crowd.

"They're unfit for freedom!" yelled a man.

The interruption spawned a fresh burst of commotion from the group, but Black quickly quieted everyone and called upon those wishing to affirm their membership in the Ku Klux Klan to step forward so he could swear them to secrecy. Several people in attendance signed on with the Klan that night, with almost everyone else expressing their agreement with the principles of the group, even if they did not feel they could become members themselves. When the sympathizers left, Reverend Jackson took part in the private swearing-in ceremony along with Stanton Black. With that the new Klansmen made their pledges, one by one, vowing to do everything in their power to undermine or destroy any black person who sought to be equal with a white person.

IN JOHNSON CITY, TENNESSEE, Ezra Justice and Nathaniel York caught another train that whisked them through the mountains, across the entire state in less than a day, and deposited them at the bustling train station in Nashville. A hotbed of spy activity for both the North and the South throughout much of the war, the streets of Nashville boasted numerous military men who still wore their Confederate or Federal uniforms, or what was left of them, and carried their weapons as they went about the postwar business of reconstruction. A lot of northern money was already flowing into the South to rebuild the war-torn towns and cities, and perhaps as a reward for its role in the war, Nashville was on the receiving end of a great deal of those early efforts. Once outside the city, however, Ezra and Nate were shocked at the devastation they saw everywhere—houses destroyed, fields burnt, and fresh crosses in every cemetery.

"We're almost home, Nate," Ezra said, as they claimed their horses from the livestock car at the rear of the train. "Just a short distance to go."

"I'm a little nervous about what we might find, Cap'n," Nate said. "But regardless, it will be home, and that's all that matters right now."

Following the trail formed by years of wagon travel, Ezra and Nate cantered along at a brisk pace, riding south for several hours, arriving in the town of Pulaski, about ten miles from the plantation. As they rode through town, Ezra noticed people staring at them—and not with friendly or curious looks. He asked Nate, "I wonder how much this town has changed in the last four years?"

"I'm sure we'll find out soon enough," Nate replied. "But right now I just want to get to the plantation and see my kinfolk."

Ezra and Nate continued riding through Pulaski and kept traveling south toward the Justice plantation. About five miles out of town, they saw two black men hanging by their necks from a tree limb. Ezra and Nate spurred their horses and raced up to the two hanging men.

They cut them down, and as they laid the two bodies on the ground, they heard a moan. Ezra and Nate turned to see another black man lying on his stomach in the grass about ten yards away. They ran to the man, and to Nate's horror, he recognized the victim.

"Ezra! This is my cousin, Abraham York. He's been shot in the back, but he's still alive."

Ezra quickly checked the wound. "The bullet is still in his back," he said. "I'll ride back to town and get the doctor. You stay here with your cousin." Ezra jumped on his horse and raced back toward town.

"Abe, who did this to you?" Nate asked as he cradled Abe's head in his arms.

"It was the men wearing white sheets, Nate," Abraham said hoarsely.

"White sheets? What are you talking about?" Nate probed.

"They wear white sheets over their clothes; and they wear white hoods over their heads, too. They look like ghosts, Nate. Those are the ones that strung up Ezekiel and Jacob, and those same ones shot me as I tried to get away.

"We went to town to see if there was any work. Some of the town folk were nice but were afraid to offer us any jobs. Several men told us to get out of town and don't come back.

"Nathaniel, we bee-lined it out of town, but these men in white sheets said we were staring at their women and that they were going to teach us a lesson." Abe coughed and winced in pain. Nate gave him a drink of water from his canteen.

"We wouldn't dare stare at the white women, Nathaniel."

"I know, Abe. I know," Nate answered, as he continued to hold Abe's head up.

When Ezra arrived in town, he didn't know where to begin to find a doctor, so he approached a stranger. "Excuse me, can you tell me where I can find a doctor in this town?" he asked. "This is an emergency."

The stranger pointed to a white house with green trim down the street. "That's Doc Evans's office right there."

"Thank you," Ezra replied, already moving in the direction of the doctor's office.

Ezra walked up to the doctor's porch just as the doctor opened the door and walked out with a patient whose arm was in a sling. "Now keep that arm stationary for at least three days," the doctor instructed the man.

"I sure will, Dr. Evans."

Ezra approached the doctor. "Dr. Evans, my name is Ezra Justice, and there's a wounded man lying on the side of the road about five miles south of town; he's got a bullet wound in his back. I was afraid to move him, so I was hoping I could bring a doctor to him."

"Let me get my bag; I'll be right with you." The doctor retrieved his black medical bag and hooked it over the horn of his horse's saddle. "I'm ready to go," he said.

"Doctor, the man is five miles down the road, on the left hand side. I'm going to get a wagon, and I'll meet you out there."

"Look, I don't know you, stranger," Doc Evans said. "How do I know that this isn't some kind of a trick?"

Ezra handed Evans ten dollars. "If it is a trick, it is an expensive trick," he said. "Now hurry, Doc!"

Dr. Evans turned his horse and headed out of town in the direction Ezra had pointed.

EZRA WENT TO THE STABLE and purchased a buckboard wagon and a team of two horses. He tied his horse to the back and drove the wagon back out the lane toward where the wounded man was still lying on the ground. When Ezra got within two miles of the location, to his surprise he saw Dr. Evans riding back toward town.

As the doctor approached him, Ezra reined the buckboard team to a stop. With the dust still swirling around him, Ezra called out to the doctor. "Doc, you could not have rendered medical attention that fast," Justice said.

"You didn't tell me the patient was a darkie," Dr. Evans snapped.

Ezra stared at the doctor with cold eyes. "Doctor, you have sworn an oath to help heal the sick and the injured. Now I'm going to swear an oath to you: if you don't turn that horse around, I'm going to shoot you out of the saddle."

Dr. Evans stared at Justice, contemplating whether he had any choices. Finally, he slowly turned the horse around and headed back to Abraham, with Ezra Justice following close behind in the buckboard wagon. They arrived back at the spot where Nate was still tending to his cousin. Nate looked up and said, "Ah, it's nice to see that you had a change of heart, Doctor." Nate smiled as he noticed Ezra's cold stare directed toward Evans.

The doctor quickly extracted the bullet from Abraham's back and put a bandage on the wound. "It missed the arteries, so he'll live," he said disgustedly, as he got on his horse and rode off toward town.

Ezra and Nate carried the two dead men over to the wagon and then helped Abe into the back of the buckboard, with Nate holding him while Ezra drove the wagon to the plantation.

Ezra drove the team slowly so Abe wouldn't be jostled any more than necessary on the way. As the horses clomped along, Nate told Ezra about the men covered in white sheets who were responsible for shooting Abe and hanging Ezekiel and Jacob. "Why would they be wearing white sheets with white hoods over their heads?" Nate asked. "What kind of strange uniform is that?"

"I don't know, Nate. But I'm going to find out."

Ezra, Nate, and Abraham York arrived within sight of the Justice family plantation just as ominous, dark clouds started rolling across the landscape. The sight of home spurred Ezra on. When he reached the peak, Ezra reined the horses to a stop. The sight that greeted him caused such a large lump to form in Ezra's throat, it nearly gagged him.

Since Nate was holding Abraham's head in his arms, he couldn't see the plantation. "How does it look?" Nate asked from the back of the buckboard.

"The plantation is in shambles, Nate," Ezra said.

Nate carefully laid Abraham's head on the floorboard of the wagon and crawled up next to Ezra. For as far as the two men could see, burned out fields stretched in front of them. Fences were torn down; a few skinny head of cattle grazed, apparently anywhere they wanted to; and off in the distance they could make out the plantation home and the out-parcel buildings, the smokehouse, the laundry house, the carriage house, the slave quarters, and the huge front lawn where Ezra and Nate had wrestled as young boys. The main house, once a stately, two-story, antebellum, Greek Revival-style home, now looked decayed and nearly unrecognizable. The smell of death and stale smoke seemed to hang in the air, even though the war had been over for months.

"Looks like we're going to have our work cut out for us, my friend," Nate said with a low whistle. "But at least we are home."

Ezra looked over at his longtime friend. "You're a good man, Nate. And I'm glad you are here with me. This is not going to be easy, but there's nothing we can't handle together. Let's head on down to the house."

The property looked even worse up close than it had from the distance. The front of the main plantation home was stained with soot and dirt. Several large indentations—each about the size of a large grapefruit—dotted the stone masonry where cannon shot had hit near the doorway. The formerly painted white brick was now blackened, and the windows were blown out. The grand foyer was now no more than a large hole in the front of the house; the door was broken, the large chandelier shattered. Behind the house Ezra could see a portion of the one-hundred-acre tobacco field that now held nothing but blackened twigs and dust.

Abe's wife, Sophie, and several other women came running when they saw the wagon. Tears of sorrow poured down their faces at sight of the two dead men. Intermingled with their sorrow were tears of relief that Abe was still alive, mixed with tears of joy at seeing that Ezra and Nate had finally returned home. As some of the plantation workers helped Abe to his cabin, other members of the family hugged Nate as though they were never going to let him go. Suddenly, they heard laughing and screaming from the main plantation house.

"What is going on in the main house?" Ezra wanted to know.

"Mr. Justice, that Mr. Donlon has been living in your house," Sophie said. "He and two men came back laughing about something. They grabbed Ophelia and took her into the house, saying they were going to celebrate."

Ezra and Nate ran toward the main house where they saw three horses still tied up out front. Passing the horses, Ezra noticed some white material protruding from a saddlebag. He opened the bag and found a white sheet and hood. He quickly checked the saddlebags on the other two horses and found similar white sheets and hoods in them. Ezra snatched the sheets out of the saddlebags and strode into the house.

John Donlon was trying to pour liquor down Ophelia York's throat as two other men held the attractive black woman by her arms.

Nate stormed over and punched Donlon square in the face, knocking him out cold. Like an angry bear, Nate grabbed the other two men by their throats and lifted them right off the ground. He threw one man in one direction and the other the opposite way, both men landing in a heap on the floor.

Ophelia York, Nate's younger sister, ran into Nate's arms, weeping. "Oh, Nathaniel, Nathaniel, I'm so glad to see you!" she cried. "I'm so glad you are home at last!"

"Did they hurt you, girl?" Nate asked.

Ophelia wiped the tears from her eyes and attempted to regain her composure, straightening her dress and rebuttoning her blouse where Donlon and his creeps had pulled it open. "No, but they were going to," Ophelia replied.

About that time Donlon stirred on the floor. "Justice." He spat out the name as he spat the blood out of his mouth, the saliva and blood mixture landing on the hardwood floor.

"What are you doing back here, Yankee? This ain't your home no more. You don't belong here."

"I'm surprised you survived the war, Donlon," Ezra replied, observing Donlon's torn, filthy Confederate uniform. "I'm sure men in both blue and gray uniforms wanted to kill you."

"You wouldn't be that lucky, Justice. Maybe Grant said that the war is over, that the Yankees and Rebels are countrymen again. But I don't feel that way. The way I see it, you deserted your brothers, goin' off to fight for the Yankees the way you did, and we don't need any Negro-lovin' traitors movin' back into town."

Ezra stood over Donlon, torn between the desire to smash his face or simply shoot him outright and save somebody else the trouble.

"Easy, Ezra," Justice heard Nate say behind him. "He's not worth it."

Justice drew back and put his hand on the LaMat at his hip. "What are you doing in my house, Donlon?"

Donlon laughed hideously. "Ha! Your house? It hasn't been your house for a long time, Justice. Your darkies did a fairly good job of keeping it up for the first few years you were gone, plantin' the crops and all. The women kept the house decent, too, 'til Hood brought his men north from Atlanta after Sherman swept through. When the Confederate Army needed food and a hospital after a few skirmishes nearby, these here floors flowed with blood."

Donlon nodded toward the hardwood floors of the large sitting room, where expensive carpets had once covered the area. Even from a distance Justice could see the dark stains, probably caused by blood.

"Ever since, this house has belonged to anyone who could keep it. The Yankees came through, too, after Chattanooga, and before they got to Spring Hill. Everybody's had a little piece of your property, Justice. Everybody but you, hey, Justice?

"And now most of your darkies are gone, too, thanks to the KKK scarin' them off, I reckon."

"The KKK?" Ezra asked.

"The Ku Klux Klan," Donlon spat out the words. "Ever hear of the Klan, Justice? They're the new law around these parts. Lincoln may have freed the slaves, and he got his for doin' it. The Klan is taking care of anyone around here that thinks them Nee-groes, as they're wantin' to be called nowadays, are equal to any white person. You can take that as a warnin', Justice."

Ezra smashed Donlon in the face, knocking him out again with one blow. "And you can take that as a warning, Donlon."

Ezra turned to Nathaniel York. "Take your sister out of here, Nate," Ezra said. "I'll take care of these three."

Ezra tied up all three men, and some of the plantation workers helped him drag them onto the back of the wagon. "I'm going to take these men to the sheriff, Nate."

EZRA ARRIVED IN FRONT OF the sheriff's office in Pulaski. He collared two of the men and dragged them off the wagon, up the boardwalk, and inside the building where he pushed them to the floor right in front of the sheriff's desk.

Sheriff Dax Cutler looked up from his desk. "What's the meaning of this?" he asked drolly.

Ezra walked out without saying a word. Outside, back at the wagon, he grabbed Donlon and carried him into the sheriff's office. Ezra dropped Donlon onto the floor, as well, right on top of the other two men.

"I asked you, mister, what is the meaning of this?" Cutler boomed.

"These three men hung two men and shot a third one in the back," Ezra said coldly.

Donlon sat up groggily on the floor and leaned against the wall. "Sheriff, come here and untie me," he called out.

"What's this man talking about, Donlon?" Cutler asked.

"This man is Ezra Justice, Sheriff. He used to own the house out at the plantation."

"Donlon, you were a scum before I left for the war, and you are still a scum," Justice said. "And you are going to hang for the murder of those two men."

"What two men?" Cutler asked impatiently.

"He's not talking about men." Donlon spat out the words. "He's talking about two darkies out there who came into town and were staring at our women."

"Oh, those two," Cutler said. The sheriff got up from his chair, reached for a knife, and cut the ropes binding the three men. "You boys get out of here," Cutler said. "I'll take care of this."

Donlon and his two friends got up and stumbled toward the door, glaring at Justice as they exited.

The sheriff walked behind his desk, sat down again, and leaned back in his chair, staring at Ezra Justice. "Now, is there anything else I can do for you, Justice?"

"Yeah, you can tell me what is going on with this Ku Klux Klan that Donlon claims to be the law around here, *Sheriff*."

"Well, Donlon is known for having a big mouth, and as far as this Ku Klux Klan, I'm the law around here. And don't you forget it."

"Are you going to do anything about the hanging of those two Negroes?" Ezra asked.

Cutler stared at Ezra and said, "I already did. Now get out of my office."

Ezra realized that Cutler was going to do nothing to bring justice to the men who had committed the hangings. The storm of discontent was only beginning.

As soon as Ezra Justice was out of sight, Dax Cutler hurried to the saloon and sat down at a table with John Donlon. "Why are you spouting your mouth off about the Ku Klux Klan, Donlon? And what were you doing out there on the plantation in the first place? Are you out of your cotton-pickin' mind?"

Donlon excitedly began telling Cutler about what happened regarding Ezra Justice and the hanging of the darkies. Cutler shook his head, got up from the table, and headed straight for Judge Stanton Black's office, barging right in without warning. "I need to see the judge right away," Cutler said to the secretary.

The secretary knocked on the judge's door and opened it slightly. "Judge, Sheriff Cutler is here to see you."

"Send him right in, Martha," Black's voice could be heard.

Sheriff Cutler walked right by Martha and went directly into the Judge's office. As soon as Martha shut the door, Cutler said, "Judge, we've got a problem. The guy who owned the plantation before the war, Ezra Justice, came into my office wanting to know about the Ku Klux Klan. He even dragged Donlon into my office, along with Jake and Pete, all three men tied up, and wanted me to arrest them for hanging those two darkies outside town!" Cutler's voice crackled with concern.

"Calm down, Cutler, and tell me the whole story."

"Those three darkies that came into town looking for work . . . I sent Donlon, Jake, and Pete out to string 'em up so no other darkies would dare come into town for work or any other reason."

"How does this Justice fellow know about what happened?" the Judge asked.

"Donlon told me that one of the darkies tried to run away, so he shot him and thought that he had killed him, but that darkie lived and told Justice all about what happened. Judge, Donlon knew Justice before the war, and he says that Justice is a man who has compassion for the darkies and will fight to stand up for their rights. In fact, even though he grew up on the plantation right down the road here, he fought for the Union, along with his darkie friend, Nathaniel York."

Cutler went on, "Donlon said that he, Jake, and Pete went back to the plantation to have a little fun with one of the young girls when Justice and York arrived home at the plantation. And they weren't too happy seeing the boys having their way with that young darkie girl.

"They found the Klan sheets that the boys had worn when they strung up the darkies earlier today. Donlon said that giant black darkie, York, just about killed him."

"Why would Donlon be stupid enough to go back to that plantation after stringing up two of the workers?" Judge Black asked pensively.

"Donlon's been living in the main house on the plantation for the last couple of years, never expecting Justice to return."

Judge Black rubbed his chin thoughtfully. "If Justice gets in the way, we may have to string up a white man. I'll pass this information on to our other senior Klan officers. Now you'll have to excuse me, Sheriff; I've got other business to attend to."

Cutler left the judge's office, knowing that the judge was the most powerful man in the county, and if Stanton Black decided to do something to deal with Ezra Justice, it would be no idle threat. Quite the contrary, it was sure to happen.

EZRA JUSTICE TOOK HIS TIME riding back to the plantation; he needed the time to think through his options. Justice realized that the opposition he was dealing with was much more serious than he could have imagined prior to returning home to Tennessee. Before the war these people looked at the Negroes as property; now they looked at them as a threat. Ezra tied up his horse at the carriage house and walked over to

Nate's cabin. The big black man was talking with his cousin, Abraham, while Ophelia fixed them something to eat.

"How are you feeling, Abe?" Ezra asked.

"I feel like I got a hole in my back, Mr. Justice, but I sure am glad to be alive," Abe answered.

"Well, just take it easy and allow yourself some time to heal," said Ezra.

"Yes, sir, Mr. Justice. A couple of days rest, and I should be fine."

"You just get to feeling better, Abe, OK?"

"Yes, sir."

"How did it go in town?" Nate asked.

"The sheriff let them go," Ezra said somberly.

"I could have told you that was going to happen," Abe said. "There are people in that town who consider us as no more than animals. If some of the white folk want to hunt down a few Negroes and string 'em up, well that's fine and dandy with them."

"Well, there's nothing we can do now," Ezra said, "but get our plantation back in order. I don't think we'll be seeing Donlon back here again anytime soon."

"Would you like some coffee, Mr. Justice?" Ophelia asked. "I just brewed a fresh pot."

"Thank you, Ophelia. That sounds pretty good right now." Ezra accepted a cup of coffee from Ophelia and sat down next to Nate. "Ophelia, I realize that things have been really tough on you and the other workers since Nate and I have been gone."

"Yes, sir, Mr. Justice. We tried to keep everything neat and clean, just like you left it, for the longest time. We cooked, cleaned, and ate our meals there in the main house on the property. Then, after a noisy battle up the road a piece, the Confederate soldiers camped out on the property. Little by little as more of them came, they started using the house. Then they turned the downstairs into a hospital, sorta. That was OK. But when they found out that they were in the home of Ezra Justice, the leader of one of the most famous units in the Federal Army, well, they seemed to snap.

"After that, they seemed to take some sort of sordid pleasure in breaking things up, even destroying things that they could have used for themselves. They wouldn't allow us back in the main house—we had to stay in our quarters—and that horrible man, that Donlon, was helping them along. He said he was going to kill you and Nate both for fightin' on the side of the North."

Ophelia wiped her tears on her apron. "Oh, Nathaniel, Mr. Justice, it was awful—the war, the fighting, the fires, the death. I've been caring for the wounded since the day they brought the first bloody soldier through those doors."

"Where's everybody else?" Nate asked tentatively, almost as though he was afraid of what Ophelia's answer might be.

"Most everyone is gone, but a few of us are still living here on the plantation. The younger ones and the older ones. The ones in the middle, the men, a lot of them joined the colored battalions. The women, those of child-bearin' years, a lot of them got swept away, carried off to who knows where, some during the war and others since emancipation became a law in these parts.

"Those people called the Klan came out here and beat some of us, and others they like to use for their own gratification."

"The Ku Klux Klan has been here?" Ezra asked.

"Oh, yes. Several times. They come around looking and asking, snooping in everywhere they can." Ophelia smiled, and her beauty seemed to blossom before the men's eyes. "They're kinda funny, with their white sheets and all. Talking real tough from under a white sheet. But then they light those torches, and it ain't so funny then. Someone said they made a cross and set it on fire the other night. I don't know what that means. All I know is that I pray every night that they won't come back."

"Should I know that fellow Donlon?" Nate asked.

"Yes, you should," Ezra said. "He was the plantation caretaker my parents fired years ago when they discovered him beating some of the male workers. We later found out that he had raped two of the young women on our plantation, as well. My parents realized they couldn't prosecute him, so they kicked him off the plantation. Donlon moved into a shack right outside our property and tried to stir up trouble as often as he could, any way he could."

"Do you think we're going to have any more trouble with him?" Nate asked.

"I'm not so concerned about Donlon; it's the sheriff I'm worried about," Ezra replied.

EZRA, NATE, AND THE REMAINING former slaves threw themselves into rebuilding the plantation. There was much to do—fences to mend, buildings to repair, and crops to plant. Over the next several weeks, a few of Ezra's farmhands who had volunteered with the Union Army returned to the plantation. The men were a welcome sight to their families who had watched them leave dressed in farm clothes, now to return wearing Federal uniforms and carrying muskets and muzzle-loaded rifles. Despite their exhausted bodies, their faces displayed a newfound confidence.

And why not? Their lives had been spared, unlike thousands of other soldiers on both sides who had gone off to war, never to return home.

Ezra Justice welcomed the men back to the plantation. "This was your home before you went off to war, and it is still your home now," Ezra told the returning soldiers. "You are welcome to stay on with us and help us rebuild the property. I'll pay you a fair wage, as best I can. There is plenty of work to be done and not a lot of time to get the tobacco and other crops planted before the weather turns. If we work together, I believe we can get this plantation back to life."

Most of the newly freed Negroes, formerly the Justice family's slaves and other employees, decided to stay on and work with Ezra Justice, the only white man they had ever truly trusted or respected. Indeed, they felt blessed to be back together.

Before long the plantation began to take shape. Working from dawn until dusk every day, Ezra and Nate and their employees soon mended the fences on the range and rebuilt the burned-out barn; they patched bullet holes in the walls of the main house and repaired some of the farm equipment that was salvageable. With lots of lye soap and water and even more elbow grease, the house started to look and smell like a home once again.

One night after supper Ezra and Nate sat on the front porch steps of the main house, talking about the strange new attitudes they were encountering now that they were home. Both men were aware that strong resentment remained toward them among ex-Confederates and their supporters in the area. "We need to be careful, Nate, not to stir things up any more than necessary," Ezra said.

"I agree, Ezra. We should keep as low a profile as possible. I heard from some of our workers that a number of the local folks are upset that you are paying former slaves fair wages to work on your property."

"Some of the local people will come to accept us. They know us; they know what kind of men we are," Ezra said. "But in the meantime it's understandable that others are angry. Tennessee experienced more battles and skirmishes during the war than almost any other state in the union, and a lot of families lost loved ones. That pain isn't going to go away in just a few days. Especially with the Ku Klux Klan out there riling people up about the freed Negroes."

"I understand, Captain," Nate said, rubbing his chin, "but it could get dangerous."

"Nate, we've been living with danger for four years. And after fighting as hard as we did for freedom, I'm not about to allow a bunch of thugs to intimidate the people I care about."

Lurking in the shadows behind some brush on the hillside above the plantation, John Donlon peered intently through binoculars, searching for any scrap of information he could pick up. Donlon smiled deviously as he noted the improvements to the plantation. *Maybe it's time for the Klan to pay Mr. Justice a visit*, he thought.

The inner circle of the Pulaski Ku Klux Klan gathered in Judge Stanton Black's office—Andrew Shaw, owner and publisher of the *Pulaski Tribune*; Dr. Howard Evans, the local physician; Sheriff Dax Cutler; and Judge Black himself. The last member, Archibald Harris, owner of the local bank, walked in late. Seeing the other members already assembled, he asked, "What's so important, Judge?"

"You're late, Arch," Judge Black said with a scowl. "But I'll reiterate what I've already told the other members. Ezra Justice is rebuilding his plantation, and he is paying darkies to work there. I see a huge problem brewing. With the success of his plantation, it will encourage other owners to move in and start treating the blacks as equals. The next thing you know, blacks will start owning plantations; then, who knows? Maybe they'll start owning banks, Arch. Or running newspapers, Andrew. Maybe they will become our sheriffs, Dax; and maybe even becoming doctors, Howard.

"Well, if you're going to go that far, Stanton, maybe some of the darkies will become judges!" The men in the room erupted in laughter. Everyone thought the comment was extremely funny, everyone except Judge Black.

"You may think this is humorous," Black said, "and it may seem ridiculous or inconceivable to you that the darkies could move into positions of authority. Certainly, we all want to treat the darkies with a bit of respect—just as we would our dogs— give them enough food to survive, provide them with shelter so they will have the energy to work. But Justice is treating the Negroes out there on his plantation as equals, and that is going too far. We've got to stop him and his kind before they pick up any momentum."

"What do you have in mind, Judge?"

"I don't know yet. Right now I just wanted to let you know what is happening. When I decide what to do, you'll be informed. Thank you, gentlemen."

The men dispersed quickly, heading back to their professional responsibilities.

SUNDAY MORNING DAWNED a beautiful day on the plantation with a crispness in the cool fall air. The work on the property was shaping up so well that Nate and Ezra felt it was safe to have a church service. The workers had converted an old barn, turning it into a genuine church sanctuary, complete with a platform and pulpit and benches for the workers to sit on during the services. A large number of workers, mostly women and children, turned out for the church service. The congregation was predominantly female because so many of the men had been killed fighting for the Union during the war; and since the formation of the Ku Klux Klan, several others had been hanged.

Nathaniel York stood behind the pulpit. Sitting on the platform back to his right was his cousin, Abraham York, the associate pastor. Ezra Justice sat in the front row with Nate's sister, Ophelia, and Abe's wife, Sophie.

Nate looked at Sophie and said, "Sophie, please come up and lead us in some songs. I need some spiritual inspiration before I give my sermon today."

Dressed in her finest blue cotton dress, Sophie stepped up onto the platform and began to sing. As she did, her eyes closed, and she leaned back slightly; her voice, clear as a bell, as strong as a trumpet's clarion call, resonated throughout the barn and beyond. Tears began streaming down her face as she sang about Jesus, not as a figure of history but as her personal friend. People in the small congregation sensed the Spirit of God in that place and stood to their feet. Many sang along; others simply closed their eyes and basked in the Lord's presence. It wasn't the first time Jesus had shown up in a barn.

Nate's sermon that morning was simple enough for a child to understand, yet the truth he conveyed from the Gospel of Matthew was deeply profound. "All of us have been hurt by somebody during this war," Nate said. "But if you allow that hurt to develop into bitterness, you will be wrapping a ball and chain around your own neck. You will be enslaved by your own unwillingness to forgive.

"The Good Book says right here in Matthew, chapter 6, verses 14 and 15, 'If you forgive men for their transgressions, your heavenly Father will also forgive you. But if you do not forgive men, then your Father will not forgive your transgressions.'" Nate paused and stepped down from the platform and walked back and forth across the barn.

"Have you ever held onto hatred or a desire for revenge?" he asked.

"Oh, yeah!" somebody shouted.

"All the time," said someone else.

Nate smiled knowingly. "And have you ever noticed that when you hold onto that ugly stuff, you have a hard time feeling God's presence in your life? It seems as though he has moved a million miles away. You pray, and your prayers don't have any effect."

"Oh," somebody said. "That's right."

Nate looked at his small congregation lovingly but sternly. "That unforgiveness will eat you up like gangrene," he said. "Let go of it. For God's sake and for your own sake, let go of it before it destroys you!"

"Amen! Amen!" several people called out.

Nate continued, "I'm not asking you to accept or condone the wrong things people have done to you. But you have to love the sinners even though you hate the sins they commit. Jesus said that if you love only those people who love you, what good is that? We are to love even those who persecute us and despitefully use us. That's God's kind of love."

Nate paused again and looked all around the barn, trying to look as many people in the eyes as possible. "Understand, I'm not asking you to feel like forgiving. I'm not asking you to condone what that person did to you or even to try to understand it. Forgiveness is a choice. It is an act of your will where you say, 'I choose to forgive that person who hurt me.' The person you forgive may not even know about it. But God will know, and you will know, and that's good enough. When you can forgive like that, you will be free indeed." Nate stepped back onto the platform.

"Come on back up here, Sophie, and lead us in a closing song."

Sophie graciously mounted the platform and began singing, slowly and softly at first and then gradually with more power and enthusiasm. "I'm so glad Jesus set me free." The congregation joined in with her. "I'm so glad Jesus set me free. Glory, hallelujah! Jesus set me free!"

The music and the message were contagious. Even Ezra Justice mouthed the words, "Jesus set me free."

A lmost immediately after the conclusion of the war, Clinton, Missouri, began receiving numerous refugees, including soldiers, immigrants, and freed Negroes—men, women, and children. Since receiving the thousand dollars from General Sherman, Elizabeth O'Banyon had taken in a black family—Rosy and her husband Jed, and their young sons Thomas, Micah, and Jonah—to help keep up the farm. Elizabeth couldn't pay them much, but she provided them with room and board. In return they helped with the farm, received some of the crops, and according to Elizabeth, provided her good company. Neither Jed nor Rosy knew how to read or write, so in the evenings Elizabeth held school for the adults and for the children.

Elizabeth longed to do more for the refugees. She and Shaun had sought refuge in America themselves after the potato crop failures in Ireland had plunged their homeland into a severe depression. Elizabeth knew firsthand what it felt like to be an outsider with no home, no money or job, and no means of support. She felt compassion for the thousands of Negroes who were now free but in some ways worse off than they'd been as slaves. She wanted to help, but she wasn't sure exactly what she could do.

One afternoon while working in her large garden, Elizabeth raised her head to wipe the sweat off her forehead. As she rested a minute, her eyes fixed on a dilapidated barn several hundred feet from the house. She and Shaun had used the old barn for their milk cows and horses but had decided to build a new barn. The old barn remained standing.

For nearly a minute Elizabeth stood in the hot sun, just staring at the old building from a distance. And then a thought came to mind that made her heart leap with excitement. She ran back toward the other side of the house, calling out as she ran, "Jed! Rosy! Come quickly!"

Jed and Rosy had been working in the field behind the house, but when they heard Elizabeth's call, they jumped to their feet and started running in her direction.

"Is somethin' wrong, Miss Elizabeth?" Jed called. "Are you alright?"

"I have an idea!"

"An idea?" Jed slowed to a jog. "What sort of idea is it, Miss Elizabeth?" He hurried across the yard and stopped in front of Elizabeth, the perspiration still dripping down his face.

"I've got it!" Elizabeth exclaimed. "Rosy, come here! I can't wait to tell you this."

Because of Rosy's round physique, she couldn't run nearly as fast as Jed, but she was slowly and surely making her way across the backyard. "Yes, ma'am," she called. "I'm a'comin'."

"Rosy, why don't you go in the house and bring us a cool glass of lemonade?"

Rosy went into the kitchen and quickly returned with a tray bearing three glasses filled to the brim. She handed Elizabeth a glass of cool lemonade and one to Jed, as well.

Elizabeth said, "Let's go out and sit down on the front porch, and I'll tell you what I have in mind. That's where my Shaun and I used to talk over our big ideas."

The three of them walked around to the front of the house and sat down on the front porch steps.

"Well," Elizabeth smiled as she spoke, "see that old barn over there beyond the garden a ways?"

"Yes, ma'am. I checked out that barn. It may be old, but it sure is solid," Jed said with a broad smile. "Whoever built that barn intended it to be here a while."

Elizabeth nodded and began again. "Well, with your help, we can fix up that old barn good enough to start a school, right here on the property."

Jed and Rosy looked at each other quizzically, then back at Elizabeth, but neither said a word.

"We've been holding a mini-school of our own after supper each night. What if we took in others who wanted to learn to read and write?" Elizabeth gushed.

"Well, Miss Elizabeth, I'm sure thinkin' that'd be mighty noble of you, but do you think we can do that, along with keepin' up with the work around here?"

"Don't you worry about that. I have enough money to hire the help we need to get it fixed up," Elizabeth O'Banyon said as she smiled. "Are you with me?"

Jed and Rosy remained silent, knowing the decision was not really theirs to make, yet appreciative of Elizabeth's willingness to include them in the process. Setter, Elizabeth's dog, bounded across the field, wagging his tail, as though wondering what all the commotion was about.

Jed looked again at Rosy and then back to Elizabeth. "Yes, ma'am, you know you can count on us. Whatever you want to do is fine with us."

Rosy nodded in agreement.

"Good, I'll go to town first thing tomorrow and hire the men to fix up the barn."

REGINALD BONESTEEL STOOD on the upper deck of the *St. Patrick* as it steamed into the docks at Memphis. It had been more than six months since he'd last been to Memphis; it seemed like a lifetime ago. A brisk wind swept across the boat, and Bonesteel grasped his collar, pulling his coat closed to fend off the cold air. Bonesteel wasn't sure whether the chills running over his body were from the fall weather or the awful memories that froze him in place as he looked out at the riverfront toward Beale Street.

In his mind Bonesteel could still see the dead bodies washing up against the shore. Some of the deceased had burned to death; many had drowned in the cold, swirling Mississippi currents after they had attempted to swim for their lives when the *Sultana*'s boilers blew up.

Bonesteel shook his head sharply as though trying to shake the horrific images from his mind. After all, this trip was meant to be a new start for him. He had actually enjoyed traveling with the lighthearted Hawkins twins from Washington to St. Louis. "The boys," as Reginald was prone to call them—though they were only a few years younger than he was—had been good company. They teased Reginald incessantly, and he pretended that he could barely tolerate their insolent remarks, but deep down inside Bonesteel liked Roberto and Carlos a great deal. He'd be willing to take a bullet for either one of them. He admired their courage and bravery in battle and their smooth, adept movements around the poker table, as well. Reginald also noticed the attractive young women that seemed inevitably drawn to the Hawkins twins. He soon realized that by traveling with the twins, his own social life expanded measurably, an added benefit of being seen with the twins that Bonesteel didn't mind a bit.

The three of them remained together in St. Louis for several weeks after their arrival in town. Bonesteel, Carlos, and Roberto had contacted Pastor Bennett and his family—Bonesteel to get another delicious home-cooked meal and Carlos to see Mary again.

At dinner Pastor Bennett told the men about the new church where everyone was welcome regardless of the color of their skin. "I knew that to open the door of the church to races other than whites was asking for trouble, so I guess we should have expected it. But I was still a little surprised when we started receiving death threats after being here only a few weeks."

"What are you going to do about it?" Roberto asked.

"Love is stronger than hatred," Pastor Bennett replied with a broad smile. "It's all in God's hands, and he's a pretty strong adversary."

Reginald Bonesteel liked the Bennett family and was impressed with their sincerity and their willingness to lay their lives on the line for God. Reginald respected that sort of commitment.

Carlos and Roberto were concerned about the danger factor so they decided to stay on in St. Louis for a while to help protect the Bennett family. Bonesteel was glad to help Reverend Bennett, too, but by the third week he was ready to move on. St. Louis was not his destination; he wanted to get out West to do some gold panning. He reluctantly said goodbye to the Bennetts and the Hawkins twins, telling them, "If you need me for any reason, you know how to get hold of me." Then Reginald Bonesteel boarded the steamer traveling from St. Louis down the Mississippi to Memphis.

Bonesteel got off the *St. Patrick*, walked down the street, and right away noticed a pretty woman dressed in a gray nurse's uniform. Gazing openly and more intently at the woman, he suddenly recognized Anna Harvey, the widow whose life the Justice Riders had saved from drowning that fateful night aboard the *Sultana*. Anna had been in Gayoso Hospital when

Justice and his men had visited shortly after the tragedy. She had lost both her husband and her baby to the river.

"Anna Harvey! Is that you?" Bonesteel asked.

"Why, Mr. Bonesteel! What a surprise! What brings you to Memphis?"

"Actually, I came on the steamer, the *St. Patrick*, and I'm on my way to California. Is that a nurse's uniform you are wearing?"

"Yes, I'm on my way home. I work at the hospital—you remember Gayoso Hospital where so many of us from the *Sultana* were brought?"

"Oh, yes, I remember it well."

"How long is your layover here in Memphis?"

"The boat leaves later this evening at ten o'clock. But Mrs. Harvey, if you have no commitments this evening, it would be my honor to take you to dinner."

"Oh, it would be my honor, Mr. Bonesteel. I owe you and your friends my life. I live at the boarding house on Beale Street. Shall we say six o'clock?"

"Six o'clock would be fine, ma'am."

Anna walked off toward the boarding house. "I'll see you then," she called with a wave.

ANNA HARVEY SPOKE QUIETLY but cheerfully as she and Reginald Bonesteel sat opposite each other in large wing-backed chairs in the exquisite dining room of the Lafayette Restaurant. "It is such a pleasure to see you, Mr. Bonesteel."

"The pleasure is all mine, Mrs. Harvey. Tell me, why did you decide to stay in Memphis?"

"Well, after being discharged from the hospital, I just could not leave," Anna said. "I was grasping onto any hope of hearing word regarding the recovery of the bodies of my husband and baby boy. I didn't want to return home to Louisville without them or without some sort of resolution in my mind as to whether their remains had been found. Bodies were still being pulled from the Mississippi River as far away as New Orleans. Perhaps some bit of news would turn up. My beloved William and our baby were my life.

"I had met and married William while I was a schoolteacher. William left to serve with the 4th Kentucky Volunteer regiment, and I had carried our child during his time away. I gave birth just three months prior to the planned trip home on the *Sultana,* a decision we felt would be safer than the train, but one that will haunt me for the rest of my life."

"I guess we all have things that will haunt us for a lifetime," Reginald said, reflecting a bit on his own gruesome experiences during the war. "So you were a teacher? Which do you prefer, teaching or nursing?"

"Well, I have enjoyed working at the hospital as a nurse, but I do love teaching. Unfortunately, there are no teaching positions open here in Memphis right now." Anna Harvey fluffed the bountiful petticoats of her chin-to-ankle dress as she spoke. "What prompts your travels to California, Mr. Bonesteel?"

Reginald smiled at Anna. "I've heard there are fortunes just waiting to be made there if one has the patience to pan for gold. I am a man of great patience, so I hope eventually to become rich and prosperous."

"I have no doubt that you will," Anna said, smiling at Bonesteel.

"And what about you, Mrs. Harvey? Do you plan to stay in Memphis?

"I don't know." Anna's expression turned contemplative. "I don't really have any reason to stay here, yet I don't have any reason to leave. I'm open to the possibilities, I suppose, and it has taken me longer than I had hoped to recover a sense of purpose. But to be honest, Mr. Bonesteel, I have grave concerns about what I am meant to do for the rest of my life. Surely, there is something to be learned from all that I have experienced, some good that can come of it, somebody that can be helped, perhaps. God must have a plan that includes me somewhere. At least I hope he does."

Bonesteel smiled, recognizing that Anna's faith went much deeper than she acknowledged. "Do you remember Captain Justice telling you about the man in the box, the casket that we were transporting home when we met aboard the *Sultana*?"

"Why, yes I do. O'Banyon, I believe, was your friend's name, was it not?"

"Yes, that is correct. Shaun O'Banyon, one of the bravest men I ever met, even if he was a bit loud." Bonesteel paused and looked toward the ceiling, as though peering into heaven. "God rest his soul . . . and his mouth."

Anna laughed aloud. "He must have been quite a character."

"He was that indeed, ma'am."

"And he had some noble friends."

"Well, yes. But the reason I mention it is that Shaun O'Banyon's wife, er . . . widow—pardon me, I'm not yet comfortable with these terms. Anyway, I've recently received a letter from Mrs. O'Banyon, and she is starting a school on her farm. Perhaps you should contact her and inform her that you are interested in obtaining a teaching opportunity. She's a spunky lady, and I think you would enjoy knowing her. I could put you in touch with her, if you'd like. Since you both have lost loved ones, she must be experiencing feelings similar to yours. Perhaps you could be of some encouragement to her and she to you."

"That's a wonderful idea, Mr. Bonesteel. If you think she and I would hit it off, I would be glad to write such a letter and ask about the job."

Bonesteel gazed at Anna, comparing her to Elizabeth O'Banyon. Anna Harvey and Elizabeth O'Banyon were nothing alike really. Anna was well-educated, articulate, soft-spoken, delicate, and petite; Elizabeth was tall, strong, as agile with a shotgun as any man Bonesteel had ever known, and a good shot, too! Elizabeth was an outdoors type of woman, willing to brand cattle and plant corn on the same day, not afraid to get dirt under her fingernails. Yet to Reginald Bonesteel, it seemed that she and Anna had a lot in common.

"I'm positive that you two will get along," Reginald said with a smile.

"It might be good therapy for me to get my eyes off my own pain for a while and recognize that others are struggling, as well. Thank you, Mr. Bonesteel, for that excellent suggestion."

Bonesteel didn't stay much longer. He and Anna shared more conversation and some tea, and then it was time for Reginald to head back to the dock to board the *St. Patrick* for the remainder of the trip to New Orleans. But before he departed, Bonesteel wrote Elizabeth O'Banyon's name and address on a scrap of paper and handed it to Anna. "Just tell her that you talked with me, and I instructed you to say 'Remember O'Banyon.' Remember those words; she will trust you immediately from there."

REGINALD BONESTEEL DEPARTED from Memphis, but his suggestion remained in Anna's mind. For more than a week she did not act on it. Then one morning Anna Harvey squinted as she looked out her window toward Auction Square. The sun was already high over Memphis and shone brightly through her second-story boarding house window. The name Elizabeth O'Banyon wouldn't leave Anna's mind that morning. Mr. Bonesteel had reminded Anna that Elizabeth was the widow of Shaun O'Banyon, the man about whom Ezra Justice had told her, the gallant Irish-born Union soldier who had given his life to save Ezra and many other men on the battlefield.

Anna was coming to grips with the harsh reality that she, too, was now a widow. Somehow her life was spared that horrible night when more than two thousand people met their deaths. The fact that Anna was still alive must have been due to a miracle from God and the actions of Ezra Justice and his men. But her husband William and her baby boy had drowned right before her eyes, taking her heart with them as they sank into the blackness of the Mississippi River.

Oh, how she had begged William not to try to go it alone, to wait for Ezra Justice and his men before diving into the cold water while holding onto their baby.

But William wouldn't listen to Anna, which was nothing new in their marriage. Stubborn as a mule, William always thought he was right, that Anna's opinion on anything didn't really matter. Sometimes his stubbornness worked to their advantage. But that same trait led to William's demise when the cold swirling water sucked him and their child to the bottom of the Mississippi.

Staying afloat with the help of a flimsy life preserver, Anna Harvey had watched in horror, helpless to do anything. The sight of her husband and baby dipping below the water and disappearing was never far from Anna's mind. She knew she couldn't dwell on the past; somehow she had to get over it. But how? How does a person "get over" such a horrific, senseless loss? Where does a person find strength to pick up and go on when every prop of security has been knocked out from under you?

ANNA TURNED FROM THE WINDOW and sat down at a wooden desk near her bed. Although she had never met Elizabeth O'Banyon, she felt a strong connection with her fellow widow, the woman who had inspired such selfless courage on the part of her husband and his friends.

"I must write Elizabeth O'Banyon a letter," she said aloud to herself. It wouldn't be much, just a small gesture from one broken heart to another, hopefully a word of encouragement, and also asking about the teaching job, whether it was still open. She could also share the fact that they held the mutual acquaintance of Ezra Justice and his friends Nathanial York and Mr. Bonesteel.

Once Anna began writing, the words poured out of her onto the paper. She wrote several pages telling Elizabeth O'Banyon about herself, including the sad story of how she had lost her husband and child. Anna went on to tell Elizabeth about her passionate desire to return to teaching. She concluded her letter:

> *I know not how long I shall remain in this city of Memphis. It is not my home, after all. In the meantime, I will attempt to stay in contact by means of letters and trust that you will do the same. I look forward to meeting you in person some day soon.*

Mr. Bonesteel emphatically instructed me to tell you, "Remember O'Banyon." No doubt, that rejoinder has some special meaning to you, so I offer it willingly.

May God's blessing be upon you,
Anna Harvey

Anna folded her letter and left the hotel to make her way to the post office, just two streets south and then west toward the river. She handed the letter to a gentleman at the counter and turned to leave when the shouts of a newspaper boy caught her attention.

"Get your copy. Read all about it!"

On a normal day Anna would discretely search for copies of the *Memphis Daily Appeal* that others had already read and left for the trash, but today she decided to splurge for a copy of her own.

"Young man, I'll take a copy," said Anna, handing the boy some coins.

"Thank you kindly, ma'am," the boy said. Anna accepted the fresh newsprint from the boy who had retrieved it from a large shoulder bag almost his size.

"You're welcome."

"Good-day, ma'am," he wished her, as he heaved the huge bag over his shoulder, back to its comfortable position on his hip.

A headline that read "Newly Formed Freedmen's League to Assist Black Waifs and Strays" caught Anna's attention. Anna stood for a moment and scanned the text. The article detailed the plight of black orphans of the war and slavery and how the Freedmen's League could assist refugees in need of clothing, food, education, and medical assistance. Anna closed her eyes and a tear trickled down her cheek as she stood on the walk outside the post office. The article had streaked through her brain and had achieved a dead center hit in Anna's heart.

She had seen the death and horror of the war. The images of the desperate faces of soldiers that horrible night aboard the *Sultana*, emaciated prisoners of war trying to get home to their families, haunted her mind. The hopeless look in their eyes as they were forced to choose between death by a burning inferno or leaping into a dark watery grave made her feel sick. She wondered how many women and children waited for their husbands and fathers, never to see them again. Many would never know what had happened to them. Her heart hurt for the many families with hope slowly turning to doubt, then eventually despair, never knowing what had become of their loved ones.

At that moment Anna felt deep down that perhaps somehow she could use her grief to help others, if only to listen and try to understand their sorrows. She had prayed that God would show her how to heal and move on with her own life. Now, as she read the newspaper article, something struck a chord in her heart. She knew that someday she would see her baby and William again, not in this world but in a better one. In the meantime she could try to help others get through their pain.

"WELL, FANCY THAT. Isn't that something?" said Elizabeth O'Banyon, as she folded the somewhat weather-worn and crinkled letter after she had finished reading. "Rosy, I think we've found our teacher."

"That is just fine, Miss Elizabeth, just fine," Rosy said as she busied herself shucking sweet corn for supper. The jovial, rotund black woman figured that if Miss Elizabeth wanted to tell her more about the letter, she would. If not, she'd just continue working on the corn.

But Miss Elizabeth was in a talkative mood today. "Rosy, do you recall that horrible tragedy of the steamship burning and sinking on the Mississippi back in April? The boat that Ezra and his men were aboard when they were bringing my Shaun after he'd been killed in battle—" Elizabeth stopped short.

It was still difficult for her to speak of her husband in the past tense. Sometimes she felt as though he were still here. His fingerprints were all over the farm, the house he'd built them, the large front porch where she and Shaun used to sit on the swing after work in the evenings, the old mining entrance that he'd turned into a shelter for Elizabeth before going off to war. But now he was gone, buried right there under one of the large shade trees. Elizabeth would be forever grateful to Ezra Justice and his men for risking their lives to bring Shaun home to be buried on the farm. Elizabeth herself had picked out the spot where the Justice Riders had buried their friend and fellow soldier, her husband and the love of her life.

"Yes'm," said Rosy, "I do remember you telling me all about that."

"Well, it turns out, according to this letter, that Ezra saved this woman's life that night, but unfortunately her husband and baby boy drowned."

"How terrible," Rosy said, instinctively putting her hands to her cheeks.

"It seems that she wrote for the simple purpose of giving me a word of encouragement, from one widow to another," Elizabeth said waving the letter in front of Rosy, as tears formed in her eyes. "But she is also a qualified teacher and would like to apply for the job."

"Sure is a small world, now," Rosy said with a nod. "I pray that the good Lord will give you both grace and peace."

"Thank you, Miss Rosy." Elizabeth smiled, something she hadn't done frequently since the death of her Shaun. "I do appreciate your prayers, Rosy. Keep 'em coming."

"Yes, ma'am, I will."

ANNA HARVEY STEPPED OFF the stagecoach in Clinton, Missouri, and realized she was in a whole new world. She looked around anxiously, her eyes searching for Elizabeth O'Banyon, who had telegraphed, saying that she would be there to meet

Anna upon her arrival. But there were no women in sight. Anna stepped onto the boardwalk and placed her heavy suitcase on the wood, trying to decide what to do.

Suddenly she heard a loud, female voice shouting, "Anna! Anna Harvey!" Elizabeth O'Banyon called out to Anna from the seat of a buckboard wagon, with the horses going at full gallop toward Anna, racing up the street of Clinton. With dust curling all around the buckboard, Elizabeth pulled on the reins and yelled, "Whoa!"

Elizabeth bounded from the buckboard, walked up, and clasped Anna's hand with a strong grip. "I am so glad to have you here, Anna! I've been your substitute teacher for far too long, and am I ever happy to have a real teacher."

"Well, thank you, Elizabeth," Anna replied, her eyes as big as saucers. "I'm . . . ah . . . delighted to be here."

"Delighted?" Elizabeth said with a nod. "Yep, you're going to make a good teacher. Now come on, let's get out to the farm, and you can get freshened up. You must be famished, and Rosy is the best cook in the territory." Elizabeth picked up Anna's heavy suitcase as though it were a toy and tossed it in the back of the buckboard.

Anna climbed on board tentatively, sat down, and attempted to straighten her dress, but it was of little use. Elizabeth was already calling, "Giddyup," and the horses jolted the wagon forward.

Ezra Justice and Nathaniel York were on their way to Pulaski to pick up some supplies. They had gone only a short distance from the plantation when they spotted a horse but no rider on the trail. They looked around and heard someone call out, "Help! Help me, please!"

Ezra and Nate rode to the edge of the road, looked down the hill, and saw a man sitting up on the ground, holding his leg. They hopped off their horses and hurried down the hill, picking their way through the brush.

As they reached the man, he called out to them, "I think I broke my leg!"

Nate knelt down beside the man, checked his leg, and said, "Yep, you've got a humdinger of a break in this leg. We've got to get you to town and get this thing set."

"I'll never make it up the hill," the injured man said. "I can't stand on my leg."

"Nope, you sure can't," Nate replied. "So if you don't mind, I'll just carry you up."

The injured man looked at Nate and said, "That's impossible."

"Not for Nate," Ezra Justice said, "Mr. . . . ah . . . ?"

"Andrew Shaw," said the man on the ground. "Publisher of the *Pulaski Tribune*."

"Well, Mr. Shaw, hang on tight." Big Nate reached down and picked up the newspaper man as though he were a child. Step-by-step Nate carried Andrew Shaw up the hill, through the brush, until they reached the road.

Nate gingerly laid Shaw on the ground. Ezra said, "I'll head back to the plantation and get the buckboard. You're not about to be able to ride a horse, Mr. Shaw."

"Do you mean . . . ?" Shaw looked at Nate. "Can't this man go get the wagon?" Shaw asked as though reluctant to be left alone with a black man.

Ezra stared at Shaw like he was ready to break his other leg.

Nate saw the fire in Ezra's eyes. "That's OK, Ezra. I'll go back and get the buckboard." Nate leaped on his horse and galloped toward the plantation.

Ezra looked at Andrew Shaw and said, "You know, mister, half of me wishes that we had left you down there."

"Look, ahh . . ." Shaw stammered, "what's your name?"

"Ezra Justice."

"Oh." Recognition dawned on Shaw's face.

"I see my name has been brought up in town," Ezra said.

"Look, Mr. Justice. It's not that we have anything against the darkies . . . ah, er . . . ah, the Negroes, but we know what is going to happen to our country if they start feeling that they are equal to whites."

"I can tell you with all sincerity, Mr. Shaw, that the man who just carried you up that hill does not want to be compared to a white person. He is his own person and proud of his heritage. You'd still be lying at the bottom of the hill if he wasn't gracious enough to carry you up."

Ezra knelt down and looked Andrew Shaw in the eyes. "Our country is changing, Mr. Shaw; and as far as I'm concerned, it is changing for the better. Now, if you decide to fight against the change, you will lose."

Neither man spoke again. Fifteen minutes later Nate raced up the road with the buckboard. He jumped off the wagon, gently picked up Andrew Shaw, and carefully laid him in the back of the buckboard. As Ezra walked by, he looked at Shaw and said, "You're lying in the same spot where two Negroes were laid after they were hung by members of the Ku Klux Klan. How does that make you feel, Mr. Shaw?"

Shaw dropped his head to his chest but didn't say a word.

Nate and Ezra transported Shaw to Pulaski, each bump in the road evoking a scream of pain from the man with the broken leg. "Can't you miss any of those bumps?" Shaw asked.

Ezra almost smiled as he hit another bump in the road; it seemed as though he were looking for them.

When they arrived in town, they pulled the wagon in front of Dr. Howard Evans's office. Nate once again lifted Andrew Shaw into his arms while Ezra walked up and knocked on the door. Evans answered the door. When he saw Ezra Justice standing there, he bristled. "What do you want?" the doctor asked harshly.

"I don't want anything from you, but Mr. Shaw does," Ezra said, turning and pointing at Andrew Shaw, as Nate carried the newspaper man into the house and put him on the bed.

Ezra and Nate turned on their heels and walked out the door. "Nate, let's go get our supplies now that we've taken care of your friend," Ezra said with a chuckle.

"My friend?" Nate said. "Very funny."

WEEKS WENT, and an atmosphere of peace and calm settled in on the Justice plantation. The plantation itself was taking on an entirely renovated look—fresh paint, new crops in the field, and an attitude of cooperation and freedom among the people working together.

"Nate, we need four more sacks of seed for the far fields. Can you send a couple of workers into town to get them?" Ezra said.

"Sure thing, Ezra. I have two young men available right here."

Henry and Amos, two teenage black workers, took the buckboard into Pulaski to pick up the seed. They pulled up in front of the general store, walked inside, and purchased four large sacks of seed. Henry stacked one sack on Amos's right shoulder and one on his left. "There you go, Amos," Henry said. "I'll get the other sacks." Amos toted the seed toward the door while Henry picked up the other two sacks. But as Amos walked out the door with the sacks of feed partially blocking his vision, two frumpy white women were walking down the boardwalk, gossiping, not looking where they were going. Amos accidentally bumped into one of the women.

Immediately, he began to apologize. "I'm so sorry, ma'am. I couldn't see you."

"How dare you! You, you . . . you darkie; you touched me!"

"I'm sorry, ma'am . . . I didn't . . ."

"Can you believe these darkies, Mabel? They think they can walk anywhere they want and just push us out of the way!"

The two women headed for the office of Sheriff Dax Cutler.

AMOS AND HENRY loaded the last two sacks of feed into the buckboard. They climbed into the front seat, and Henry picked up the reins, preparing to leave town and return to the plantation.

Just then the sheriff walked up with the two women. "Which one of them did it, Ozelle?"

"Which one was it, Mabel? I can't tell one from the other!" the woman sneered.

"I think it was that one," Ozelle said, pointing at Amos.

Sheriff Cutler reached up and jerked Amos off the wagon. "Come on, boy, yer comin' with me." He marched Amos off to the jail.

Frightened out of his mind, Henry took off with the buckboard, racing the distance back to the plantation. From the carriage house where he was shoeing a horse, Nate saw Henry's team of horses galloping onto the grounds, the buckboard tossed from side to side over the dusty road, the sacks of feed bouncing in the air with each bump.

Still wearing his branding apron, Nate dropped the horseshoes and came running. "What's wrong, Henry? Where's Amos?"

Henry could hardly talk, he was shaking so badly, but Nate finally got the information out of him.

"They, they . . . they took Amos to the jail. They're probably gonna hang him!" Henry rasped.

"Jail? What? Why would they want to hang him?"

"Some woman said that he touched her. Amos was carrying the seed out of the store, and he didn't see her. He accidentally bumped into her. Oh, Mr. Nate. They're gonna hang him, I know for sure!"

Ezra Justice came out of the house, and Nate informed him about what had just happened. Ezra looked at Nate. "I'll go in and find out what is going on."

"This could be a setup, Ezra. Be careful."

Ezra mounted his horse and headed for town. Nate called out to him as he went, "If you're not back in three hours, Ezra, I'll be coming for you."

EZRA BURST INTO DAX CUTLER'S JAIL and saw the deputy sheriff sitting with his feet propped up on Cutler's desk, but the cell was empty. "Where's the young black boy?" Justice demanded to know.

"That darkie is already in the courthouse," Cutler's deputy said, "getting himself ready to be hung."

Justice left the jail and rushed to the courthouse. The court was already in session, with the sheriff standing next to Amos. Mabel, his accuser, was on the stand testifying how Amos had accosted her. "It's amazing how these darkies are so attracted to white women," Mabel said, fanning her neck. "They should stick to their own kind."

As Ezra Justice walked into the courtroom, Judge Stanton Black glared at him. Everyone turned to see what had captured the judge's attention. "What do you want, Mr. Justice?" Black demanded to know, interrupting Mabel's testimony.

"I see a prosecuting attorney," Ezra said, "but I don't see a defense attorney."

"There was no time to get one," Stanton Black said, "and besides, there is no need."

"Let me be the judge of that," Ezra said. "I'll represent the young man."

"You mean the darkie."

"I mean the young man," Ezra stated firmly.

The prosecuting attorney called out, "I protest, Judge!"

"Protest all you want, Mr. Prosecutor, but in America the laws say that a man is entitled to a defense attorney," Justice said. "Otherwise, this whole procedure is a farce."

"Be my guest, Mr. Justice," Judge Black said with a smirk on his face.

Ezra walked to the front of the courtroom and stood in front of Mabel. "Are you the lady making these accusations?" he asked.

"They aren't accusations! They are the truth!"

"Alright. Let's find the truth," Ezra said. "What were you doing at the time when you claim the accused touched you?"

"I was walking down the boardwalk with Ozelle, talking about raising funds for our women's quilting society."

"So you were really engrossed in your conversation." Ezra turned away from Mabel and looked toward several women in the audience. "Is that right, Ozelle?"

"Yeah! We sure were!" Ozelle answered impulsively.

"Ozelle, you are not on the stand," Judge Black rebuked her.

"Oh, sorry, Your Honor."

"So you were so excited about raising money for the women's quilting society that you really weren't looking where you were going, were you, Mabel?"

"Well, ah . . ."

"Now, Mabel, you're under oath," Justice reminded her. "And you wouldn't want God to strike you down, now would you? Now think about this, Mabel. Were you looking at Ozelle talking when that man walked out the door? And you bumped into each other? So it really wasn't either person's fault."

Mabel looked up toward Judge Black. "It could have been something like that."

Ezra looked straight at Stanton Black and said, "Mabel has said under oath that she was as much to blame as this young man. Now I firmly request that you do your duty as a judge and dismiss this case."

Judge Black glared at Justice.

Justice's eyes locked on Black's as he said, "Dismiss it, Judge, or I will."

Judge Black continued staring at Justice, silently trying to decide how far he could take this.

Ezra wasn't going to wait any longer. He turned and walked over to where the sheriff was standing next to Amos. Justice stared the sheriff right in the eyes with his hand resting on the butt of his LaMat. His eyes never leaving Cutler's, Ezra spoke to Amos. "Come on, Amos."

Amos got up and started walking toward the door, scared out of his britches.

Ezra waited a moment to see if the sheriff would make a move. Cutler didn't. He could see in Justice's eyes that he was not a man to fool with. Cutler knew deep down that if he made a move on Justice, he would not see the light of another day.

Justice walked out of the courtroom, knowing that this would not be his last encounter with the sheriff or the judge.

The plantation was flourishing, so Ezra felt that it was time to replenish the livestock and finish off the work on the main house. "We need some building materials and furniture for the house, Nate, but what we need, Pulaski can't supply. Let's take the buckboard over to Lewisburg; it is a little farther, but we will be able to obtain the things we need. We'll need a couple of workers to go with us, so let's take Henry and James."

"Yes, Amos is still getting over his last encounter in town," Nate said with a laugh.

"Let's leave in about an hour," Ezra said.

ON A HILLSIDE ABOVE THE PLANTATION, John Donlon looked through his binoculars that were trained on the property, wanting to see how far along the workers were on the repairs. Donlon watched with interest as Ezra, Nate, and two workers headed out toward Lewisburg. Donlon jumped on his horse and raced back to Pulaski.

"Justice and three darkies just left the plantation in their wagon, heading toward Lewisburg," he told Sheriff Cutler. "It looks like they are getting their supplies there this time."

"Thanks, Donlon, I'll take it from here."

Dax Cutler wasted no time in going to see Judge Black. "You wanted me to let you know when Justice left the plantation. Well, he is gone. Took three darkies with him, and it looks like they're on their way to Lewisburg."

"Alright. Gather the men, and get them ready to ride."

ON A SATURDAY EVENING Abe York announced a special church service at the makeshift church to celebrate the progress on the plantation. Since Nate had accompanied Ezra, Abe stood on the platform, leading the service and speaking to the congregation.

"We are so blessed to have gotten this far on the renovations of our homes and property. How good God has been to allow Mr. Justice and Mr. Nate to return to us safely. This is a new dawning for all of us. Maybe now that the war is over we can get back to dreaming about what God has for us and what he wants us to do."

Abe paused to let his listeners get the full impact of his words.

"Preach it now," someone called from the side seats in the barn.

"Understand," Abe said, "there's a dirty old man trying to destroy you."

The audience sat in rapt attention, waiting to hear who the person was that Abe felt was so dangerous.

"The apostle Paul said that there's a dirty old man inside, your sinful nature, the old you, who was enslaved not by masters, not by the government, but enslaved by sin!" Abe's voice grew louder as large drops of perspiration formed on his forehead.

"That's why the apostle says that we are to lay aside the old self, which is being corrupted with the lusts of deceit, and be renewed in the spirit of your mind."

"That's right," an elderly black woman said. "Hallelujah!"

"And put on the new self, which in the likeness of God has been created in righteousness and holiness of the truth!"

Several men and women in the congregation stood to their feet, raised their hands, and started waving their arms from side to side.

"Don't let the devil deceive you any longer!" Abe cried out. "Don't accept his dirty impressions of who you are. You are a child of God. And he wants to give you his power to live the way he intended you to live."

Choruses of amens floated throughout the barn.

Just as Abe was nearing the end of his sermon, twelve Ku Klux Klan members rode onto the plantation. They charged into the church and grabbed Amos, saying, "You cheated justice once, darkie; you won't a second time! We're going to hang you right here on this plantation."

Abe stepped from behind the pulpit and ran to defend Amos. "You can't do that!" he shouted at the Klansmen. "You have no right to be here."

"I'll tell you what we can do," the leader of the white-sheeted group said. "We can hang you right along with him! Grab him, boys."

Several strong hands latched onto Abe's arms, dragging him out of the church along with Amos. Two other men threw two ropes over a large hanging tree in the middle of the plantation. The plantation workers screamed, begging the KKK not to do such a horrible thing, but the Klansmen carried on.

Sophie ran to Abe, clutching his arm, trying desperately to pull him out of the grasp of the Klansmen. One of the men covered by a white sheet punched the petite woman in the face, knocking her to the ground. Blood spewed from her mouth and down the front of her dress.

"Sophie!" Abe screamed. Two Klansmen looped a noose around Abe's and Amos's necks. As they started to pull them up, Abe screamed, "I love you, Sophie!"

"Don't leave me, Abe!" Sophie wailed from the dirt where she had fallen.

"And I love you, Jesus!" Abe called out, looking heavenward as the noose began tightening on his neck. The Klansmen jerked on the ropes, pulling Abe's and Amos's feet off the ground, causing them to hang by their necks in midair, between heaven and earth. The men in white sheets tied the ropes around the tree to secure them. Then the Klansmen climbed onto their horses, and one of them yelled, "Next time we will hang all of you if you don't leave this plantation.

"Burn this barn they call a church. And burn the main house, too," the leader called out to the other Klansmen. The men on horseback rode by and threw their lit torches into the church and into the home of Ezra Justice. They sat on their horses watching until the fires had caught sufficiently that the workers would be unable to extinguish the flames. "Let's get out of here," the leader ordered, as the men rode off the plantation, which was rapidly turning into an inferno.

General William T. Sherman, along with a contingent of officers, rode up the trail onto the O'Banyon farm, heading toward Elizabeth's house. Setter, the O'Banyons' dog, had been lying drowsily on the porch; but when he heard the horses approaching, he immediately leaped to his feet and started barking. He ran off the porch toward the soldiers, running in circles around the horses, barking at each one as though he was trying to let them know who was boss around the O'Banyon farm.

Elizabeth knew they were coming. General Sherman's staff had informed her of the special visit by the general. Standing on the front porch, dressed in a long flowing dress, her strawberry blonde hair blowing in the gentle breeze, Elizabeth looked absolutely radiant as the officers rode up to the front porch.

General Sherman reined his horse in front of the house. He dismounted and walked toward the porch. He removed his hat, then his riding glove, and stepped up to meet Elizabeth for the first time face-to-face. He reached out his hand and took Elizabeth O'Banyon's hand in his own. "I am honored to be in your presence, madam," Sherman said, as he leaned over and kissed Elizabeth's hand. "I am sorry for the loss of your dear husband. From everything I have heard about him, he was a man of great character and inner strength, two qualities that I understand are equally applicable to you."

"Why, thank you, General Sherman. It is I who am honored that you—the commanding officer of the Federal Army—would come all the way across the country to grace our property with your presence. My Shaun would be a proud man today."

"We need more men like your husband," Sherman said, finally relinquishing Elizabeth's hand. "Brave men who are willing to sacrifice their own well-being for the benefit of others. Men and women who are not afraid to stand up for what is right. You can be proud, Mrs. O'Banyon, to have shared a man such as Shaun O'Banyon with the United States of America. He gave his life for the sake of others, and he did not die in vain. Captain Justice and his men are alive today because of the sacrifice your husband made, and the war has ended that much sooner because of the contributions those men have made to our country."

"I appreciate your kind words, General," Elizabeth answered graciously. She lowered her head for a moment almost as though she were praying. She brushed away a tear from her eye, and she raised her face with a smile. "You men must be tired and in need of some refreshments. Please come inside, and we will serve you something to eat and drink. Rosy, Jed!" she called back toward the house.

The roly-poly, smiling black woman appeared at the screen door. "Yes, Miss Elizabeth?"

"Please prepare some refreshments for these gentlemen; and Jed, come help the officers find water and hay for their horses." The slender black man bounded out the door and headed toward the horses. "Yes, ma'am, Miss Elizabeth," he said respectfully.

Jed took the reins of General Sherman's horse, as well as Lieutenant Bailey's and two other officers', as the men began walking with Elizabeth toward the house. The rest of the soldiers in Sherman's contingent stayed mounted and followed Jed back toward the barn.

Elizabeth O'Banyon walked between General Sherman and Lieutenant Bailey as they stepped onto the porch and into the house.

Anna Harvey walked down the stairs of the house as the entourage entered. Elizabeth said, "General, I would like you to meet a special friend of mine who is also the principal of our new school here on the farm, started in honor of my husband. Gentlemen, this is Anna Harvey."

"It is a pleasure to meet you, gentlemen," Anna said demurely.

The officers shook Anna's hand. "The pleasure is mine," one after another said, admiring Anna's radiant beauty.

After a brief time of refreshments, the entire group gathered in the living room of Elizabeth O'Banyon's home. On the fireplace mantle was a picture of Shaun O'Banyon together with Elizabeth. It was a larger version of the picture Shaun had carried next to his heart in a locket until the day he died. Ezra Justice had returned the locket to Elizabeth, and she had worn it every day since that time.

Rosy and Jed brought in chairs from the dining room so the hosts and guests could sit around the room in a circle, facing one another. When everyone had gathered, General Sherman stood to his feet.

"We don't really have a protocol for this sort of thing, Mrs. O'Banyon," Sherman began, "since these ceremonies are usually conducted by the President at the White House in Washington. But allow me to express once again, on behalf of the President of the United States, the Secretary of War, and myself, just how deeply indebted we are to your husband for his outstanding and sacrificial service to our country."

Elizabeth sat in one of the dining room chairs, her feet together solidly on the floor, her hands folded in her lap. She looked as though she were sitting in church or at the theater as she listened intently to the general. Setter lay at Elizabeth's feet. Next to Elizabeth sat Anna, Rosy, and Jed and their boys. Elizabeth wanted them all to share in this ceremony, so Rosy had dressed the boys in white shirts and ties and their best church clothes. The remainder of the Sherman entourage filled in behind the circle.

General Sherman took a deep breath and began reading from a formal-looking paper bearing the seal of the United States of America:

Dear Mrs. O'Banyon.

The government of the United States of America wishes to inform you that the President and the Congress have honored your late husband, Sergeant Shaun O'Banyon, by awarding him the Congressional Medal of Honor for his gallant bravery in battle.

As you may know, the Congressional Medal of Honor is the highest award given by our nation to military personnel for meritorious action. Mrs. O'Banyon, I am sure your grief at the loss of your husband is beyond consolation, but rest assured, your husband's sacrificial actions resulted in saving the lives of numerous Federal soldiers, including those in his unit and at least twenty other soldiers. You can be eternally proud of him.

William Stanton
Secretary of War

"What a wonderful letter, Elizabeth!" Anna gushed. "And what a great honor for your husband and for you."

"There's more," General Sherman said. "Here is another document certifying this special award." Sherman showed the parchment certificate to the group and then read it aloud:

To all who see these presents, Greetings:
This is to certify that the President of the United States of America, pursuant to acts of Congress approved July 12th 1863, has awarded to Sergeant Shaun

O'Banyon the Congressional Medal of Honor for actions against an armed enemy of the United States.

Given under my hand this 15th day of October 1865.

Andrew Johnson, President

Rosy looked at Jed. "The President!" she said. "Imagine that, Jed. The President saying something so nice about somebody we know."

General Sherman removed the large, gold imprinted medal attached to a red, white, and blue ribbon-like necklace from the mahogany jewelry box in which he was carrying it. "Mrs. O'Banyon, it is my distinct honor to present this Congressional Medal of Honor to you on behalf of your husband."

Elizabeth rose and stepped in front of General Sherman as the general placed the ribbons over her head, the medal falling to the center of her chest. "I am extremely honored, General," Elizabeth spoke quietly but clearly. "I will cherish this medal always, as a reminder of the truth by which my dear husband lived and died: 'Greater love hath no man than this, that a man lay down his life for his friends.' That word comes from the Gospel of John, chapter 15, verse 13. When I think about the sacrifice my Shaun made, it reminds me of the sacrifice Jesus made, giving his life for us, his friends. And it motivates me to open my home, my property, and my heart to those around me who may not be as fortunate as I am. That's why I am so glad that Anna is here to help with the school."

Elizabeth nodded toward Anna Harvey, and Anna nodded back with tears in her eyes.

"And I am so grateful for Rosy and Jed and the boys. We could not have gotten the school ready without your help." Elizabeth took Rosy's hand as she spoke.

"And of course, I owe a debt of thanks to Ezra Justice and his men, who brought my Shaun home and without whom I would not have known about the sacrifice my Shaun made for us.

"This Medal of Honor does not belong to me," Elizabeth continued. "It belongs to all of us. I am going to place it in a shadow box and have it framed as a constant reminder of our mission in life: to help as many people as possible and to point them to our heavenly Father, who gave his only Son, that we might live. Thank you, once again, General Sherman. I am deeply honored by this presentation."

Elizabeth sat down with her eyes closed and head bowed. Tears flowed freely down the faces of Anna, Rosy, Jed, and the boys. Even General Sherman's young officers had tears welling in their eyes as they stood at attention.

14

"W atch those bumps, Henry," Nate said. "We don't want any of the furniture to fall out."

"I'm doing my best, Mr. Nate," Henry said.

"You're doing fine, Henry. Don't worry about it. We're almost home," said Ezra.

The group rounded the turn leading up the trail to the Justice plantation. As they neared the main house, they realized that something was seriously wrong. "Where is everybody?" Nate wondered aloud. Nate and Ezra spurred their horses and started riding hard toward the main property. As they drew closer, they could hardly believe their eyes!

The church had been burned to the ground, and the main Justice home had been burned down as well. Two ropes hanging from a nearby tree told the story.

Ezra and Nate rode to the center of the main property, and when the workers saw them, they began coming out of their cabins, crying as they walked toward the area where the main house had stood proudly for so many years.

As Henry and James pulled up in front of the carriage house, Sophie told Ezra and Nate, "A group of men dressed in white sheets, white hats, and masks took Abe and Amos to that tree over there and hung them. Nate, my Abe tried to stop them from hanging Amos, but they grabbed him and hung him, too. They burned the church and your house, Mr. Justice. There was nothing we could do. They told us that if we didn't leave, they were going to hang all of us next."

"Nate, I'm going to Pulaski," Ezra said.

"Pulaski? Ezra, you can't take them all on by yourself."

"I don't intend to," Ezra answered as he rode off.

EZRA RODE TO PULASKI, never slowing down until he reached the front of the telegraph office. He went inside and said to the telegraph operator, "I want to send a telegram to Elizabeth O'Banyon in Clinton, Missouri."

"Yes, sir," the operator said as he prepared to scribble on a piece of paper. "Send this," Ezra said:

NEED ALL J. R. REMEMBER O'BANYON!

"And sign it, 'Ezra Justice'."

When Ezra walked out of the telegraph office, Sheriff Cutler and five of his men were standing there waiting for him. "Now that you don't have a home, Justice, I figure you will be packing up and leaving right soon. Am I right?" Cutler said.

Ezra glanced up at the tops of the buildings across the street and noticed several men with rifles aimed at him.

"Of course, if you have something else in mind, . . . why don't we settle it right now?" Cutler seemed to be tempting Ezra to go for his guns.

"Cutler, you are a poor excuse for a sheriff. One day you will pay for violating your oath of office." Ezra pushed past Cutler; he mounted up and rode out of Pulaski.

Cutler bounded up the steps and burst into the telegraph office, slamming the door behind him. "What did he say in his telegram, Sam?" Cutler demanded of the telegraph operator.

Sam looked at the piece of paper on which he had scribbled Justice's note. "He said, 'Send all J. R. Remember O'Banyon.'"

"That's all he said?" Cutler wanted to know.

"That's it, Sheriff. Honest."

"What does he mean by that, I wonder?" Cutler said out loud.

"Beats me, Sheriff," Sam said with a shrug of his shoulders.

Cutler stormed out of the telegraph office. "Remember O'Banyon, huh? I'll give Justice something to remember."

ELIZABETH O'BANYON AND ANNA HARVEY walked up the boardwalk in Clinton, looking in the windows as they walked. "We need to stop in the telegraph office," Elizabeth said, "to see if I've heard from any of our boys." She and Anna stepped inside the office and over to the grated window.

"Good afternoon, Mr. Jones. Any messages for me?" Elizabeth asked, as she did most every day.

"As a matter of fact, you do have a telegram waiting for you right here." The kindly Mr. Jones retrieved the yellow envelope from behind the counter and handed it to Elizabeth.

Elizabeth read the telegram, and Anna could see the concern on her friend's face. "Is there a problem, Elizabeth?"

"I'm afraid there is, Anna. Mr. Jones, I need to send out three telegrams right away."

Reginald Bonesteel arrived in San Francisco after a long, arduous trip cramped aboard a steamship that had embarked from New Orleans. He waited patiently with Captain Bartholomew Stephens while the ship's crew worked to lower the gangplank so the passengers could disembark. "No offense intended, Captain," Bonesteel told Captain Stephens, "but I can hardly wait to get off your boat. It has been an extremely tiresome journey."

"No offense taken, Mr. Bonesteel," Captain Stephens replied. "You've handled the trip better than most. Of course, it could have been worse. We could have taken the longer water route to California. That's about seventeen thousand miles around South America and takes between five and seven months," Captain Stephens said with a laugh.

"No, thank you," Bonesteel said. "I'm glad I chose the quicker route—across Panama—although it was much more expensive and nearly depleted my military mustering-out pay.

But it was worth it. I'm here in California, and I'm ready to make my fortune in gold."

"Well, good luck to you, Mr. Bonesteel," Captain Stephens said with a slight chuckle. "But let those ships out there in the harbor be a warning to you." The captain raised his arm and pointed.

Bonesteel peered in the direction the captain was pointing. He was surprised to see dozens of large ships abandoned in the San Francisco harbor.

"What happened here?" he asked the captain. "Why are there so many decaying ships lying in these waters? Was there some sort of naval battle waged along these shores?"

"No, my friend," Captain Stephens said, placing one hand on Bonesteel's shoulder and pointing with his other hand out at the harbor. "All of those ships that you see—or at least those that haven't yet been dashed to pieces by the surf—were abandoned when their crews went searching for gold.

"At one time there were close to six hundred ships in the harbor off these shores. These that you see are some of those left over from the gold rush in 1849. A lot of those foolish sailors thought they were going to find gold as soon as they got off the boat. They didn't realize that the gold was still another 150 miles inland!"

Captain Jones shook his head sadly. "By the time they actually got to where the gold could be found, they were exhausted, hungry, and had spent their last dollar. Many of them never returned to their ships."

"I'll keep that in mind," Bonesteel said, as he picked up his rifle and hoisted the knapsack carrying all his earthly possessions over his shoulders. "Thank you, Captain, for a most interesting ride."

"Do be careful out there, Mr. Bonesteel," the captain said. "It is a rugged existence in the gold fields, and true friends are hard to find when there is so much wealth at stake."

"I understand. I'll keep my eyes wide open," Bonesteel promised.

REGINALD BONESTEEL continued his journey by railroad to Sacramento and eventually on horseback to Grizzly Flats, a small mining town south of Placerville, California, in El Dorado County about thirty miles outside Sacramento. He'd been directed to Grizzly Flats by Dooley Corrigan, an Irish old-timer who had been prospecting there since John Sutter and James Marshall had first found gold in the area back in January 1848.

Dooley Corrigan had staked his claim in Grizzly Flats shortly after that. Now, more than eighteen years later, long after many of the forty-niners had either made their fortunes or given up in frustration, Dooley remained steadfast. He'd found enough gold fragments to make a living, and he was convinced there was a vein of gold running somewhere on his property. He wasn't leaving until he found it.

Reginald Bonesteel met Dooley when the old-timer traveled to Sacramento to register his finding of a good claim, which included several chunks of gold nuggets as well as some gold fragments and a handful of flakes, at the district mining office. Reginald Bonesteel had just arrived in Sacramento and was standing in line behind Dooley Corrigan, so the two men struck up a conversation.

"If a fellow were just arriving on the scene and didn't really know where to start prospecting, good sir, where would you suggest he begin?" Bonesteel asked.

Dooley Corrigan eyed Reginald Bonesteel cautiously. It wasn't safe to give out too much information to strangers. Claim jumpers lurked in every corner these days, just waiting to see who they could rob or intimidate into leaving a good claim. Lawrence "Buck" English and his gang had made a comfortable living by encroaching on claims that other men had worked hard to find. But for some reason, Dooley felt that he could trust Bonesteel. "Aye, you say you're just joining the party, hey, is that it?" Dooley asked. "Where have you been all these years?"

"Well, sir, I've been rather busy fighting the war back east," Bonesteel replied.

"Yes, that would slow you down a bit. Well, you're here now. That's all that matters."

"Is there really as much gold out there as everyone says?" Bonesteel asked Dooley.

"Oh, yes, there's plenty of gold. Don't worry, son," Dooley Corrigan reassured Bonesteel. "This is gold country. You'll find your share if you work hard, stick with it long enough, and if Lady Luck is on your side."

"Well, I feel lucky, and I'm willing to work," Bonesteel said. "I'm just not certain where I should focus my efforts."

Dooley Corrigan cocked his head sideways as he pulled on the suspenders holding up his mining pants, the legs of which were tucked inside knee-high boots. "Tell you what, young man," he whispered. "There's a spot just down river from me, where I'm almost positive you can find some gold. All you need is a pick and a shovel, a good pan, and a lot of patience, and the gold will practically come to you."

"Really?"

"Have I ever lied to you before, lad?" Dooley asked with feigned audacity and a twinkle in his eye. "Look here," he said quietly, opening a leather pouch and showing Bonesteel the contents. "I found these stones right above the spot I'm telling you about. I think there's a lot more where this came from."

Bonesteel could hardly believe his eyes. Inside the pouch were three nuggets of gold, each about the size of a silver dollar. Bonesteel had no idea how much the gold was worth, but no doubt it was a lot. And he figured that it had to be dangerous carrying that much gold around in a pouch like that.

"My good man, that must be a fine claim you have there," Bonesteel said, raising his eyebrows and nodding his head.

The old-timer smiled through his coarse, bushy beard and mustache. "You'll find yours. Come with me; I'll help you."

Dooley Corrigan helped Bonesteel stake a claim and to get established in Grizzly Flats. He showed Bonesteel how to search for gold and how to swirl the water in his pan just right to avoid losing any tiny gold fragments that could otherwise be easily swished out with the muddy water.

"The river erodes the rock and washes the gold from the rock and other deposits, carrying it downstream," Dooley explained. "The heavier gold sinks to the bottom of the silt. That's why you can never give up on an area. There may be gold lying in a sandbar today that wasn't there yesterday. It never hurts to check." Dooley grinned. The old-timer seemed to enjoy teaching the much younger Bonesteel some of the secrets of prospecting.

Bonesteel was a quick study, too. He threw himself into the work with a reckless abandon, panning for gold from dawn till dusk every day but finding little more than enough to pay for his food.

Day after day Reginald Bonesteel knelt down in the mud next to the rippling stream, his pant legs getting soaking wet, the red clay making a permanent imprint on his knees. Bonesteel didn't care. His eye had caught a glimpse of something sparkling in the cold mountain water, running only about six to eight inches deep in the spot where he was looking. The Brit's heart beat a little faster as he scooped up some sand and mud in a twelve-inch pan and began to slowly swirl the water around in a circle, sifting the water and the sand and allowing any excess water to splash out over the side, leaving the stones and hopefully the precious metals to drop to the bottom of the pan. But all he found were pebbles.

Like most of the other prospectors, he lived in a small canvas tent near the stream and cooked his meals over an open campfire, his diet consisting mostly of beans, bacon, and whatever game he was able to shoot.

It was a lonely existence for Reginald Bonesteel, especially after living so closely with the Justice Riders. Most prospectors maintained a healthy suspicion of one another, so they kept their friendships at arm's length; neither did they allow themselves to get too close to anybody. After all, even a so-called friend might succumb to temptation if he thought there was a cache of gold nearby. More than a few "friends" had been found floating facedown in the river after someone stole their gold or encroached upon their claim.

Consequently, many miners who stayed isolated, much to themselves, suffered from homesickness as well as physical ailments from lack of good food and sleeping on the cold, damp ground. Sanitation was poor, and the miners seldom bathed or washed their clothes. Many prospectors came to Grizzly Flats alone; they lived alone and died alone. They did, however, get together for occasional card games and gambling. Despite the repugnant personal hygiene of most of his fellow prospectors, Reginald Bonesteel often took part in the poker games, hoping to win enough money to pay for supplies. Dooley even joined in a game every now and then.

While most everybody in the small town of Grizzly Flats was friendly, the only person Bonesteel really trusted was Dooley Corrigan. And Dooley was a constant source of knowledge and encouragement to Bonesteel. "This is where the mother lode lies," Dooley told Bonesteel one day after the Brit had panned since sunup with nothing to show for it. "Don't get discouraged, son," Dooley said. "Most people don't get rich overnight. It takes some time. But don't fret; there's plenty of gold left. Everyone thinks all the gold is gone, that the rush is over. But at least three-quarters of the mother lode is still in the ground! There are new nuggets and flakes floating downstream all the time, too, enough for the likes of you and me to get plenty rich."

"I keep looking and trying to find some of those flakes and nuggets," Reginald Bonesteel said, the discouragement obvious in his voice. "But I haven't found a thing worth keeping yet. I've been here for several weeks now. All I have to show for it are some pretty stones and a nagging cough. I felt certain that I'd have made my fortune by now. I had heard all those stories of prospectors finding gold lying in the streambeds just waiting to be picked up."

"Yep, some do," Dooley said, stroking his bushy beard. "I've seen some younguns pull into town, stop off at the mine supply store, get themselves a pan, stick it in the water, and pull up enough gold to live a lifetime. In the early days gold was easy to find. You could pry it right out of the rocks. And a lot of prospectors did. But for most of us, the process is slower. And I'm glad it is. I enjoy the anticipation of the search."

Dooley Corrigan was a true prospector; he didn't care so much about getting rich from the gold as he did about finding it. Nevertheless, other people who knew where Corrigan's claim was located constantly tracked Dooley's trips to Sacramento, attempting to discern when the old-timer had found something worth registering. More than one claim jumper had tried to run Dooley off his place along the riverbank.

Reginald Bonesteel was almost nodding off to sleep in his tent one night when he heard some shots that sounded as though they came from upriver. Bonesteel grabbed his Henry long-range rifle, ran outside in the brisk California night air, and headed toward Dooley's campsite in the dark.

Bonesteel stopped short of Dooley's camp and crept through the tall pine trees along the river toward Dooley's tent. He got close enough to see two young men ransacking Corrigan's possessions, tossing the old man's things out by the fire. Dooley was tied to a tree nearby. "Where's the gold, old man?" one of the men shouted in Dooley's face.

"Right there in the stream. Pan for it!" Dooley answered.

The young man kicked Dooley in the stomach, causing his head to lurch backward and ricochet off the tree behind him to which he was tied. "We heard in town that you found plenty of gold, so you better tell me, old man, or I'm gonna beat you till you do."

When Bonesteel saw that Dooley had already been beaten badly, he let his emotions get the better of him. He stepped out of the thicket and shouted, "You've done all the kicking you're gonna do. Now step away from him!" Bonesteel pointed the Henry right at the two men.

The two claim jumpers slowly eased in opposite directions, spreading out so Bonesteel wouldn't have a clean shot. "You can't shoot both of us," one of them sneered.

"Oh, you have no idea what I can do," Bonesteel said coldly. "I'm just trying to decide which of you I should shoot first. Maybe you will be my first shot since you have the biggest mouth."

The man who had talked so boldly to Bonesteel seemed hesitant. "Porter, as soon as he points that rifle at me," the mouthy man said, "go for your gun and drill him!"

"Yeah, Porter," Bonesteel said, "you do that. But I'm tired of talking. Either go for your guns or get out of here."

As though reading each other's minds, both claim jumpers went for their guns at the same time.

But Bonesteel shot Porter first, then did a dive-and-roll maneuver, cocking his rifle as he tumbled, with a spate of bullets flying over his head. Bonesteel rolled to his knees and shot Mr. Mouthy in the chest, killing the second claim jumper instantly.

Bonesteel ran over to Dooley and began untying his ropes. "Are you OK, Dooley?" Bonesteel asked.

"I'm fine," Dooley replied, as he stood up and shook off the last rope that had bound him. "I must be getting old, letting those two scallywags sneak up on me like that." Dooley shivered from the cold.

"Come on, Dooley. Let's get you warmed up," Bonesteel said, as he helped the older man over to the fire. Bonesteel and Corrigan put a pot of coffee on the fire to brew, and while they were waiting, the two men warmed themselves by the fire. They talked for a while, and Bonesteel confessed his disappointment to Dooley. "I'm a patient man, Dooley, but my patience is running out. I surely thought I'd have found a bit of gold by now."

"Just give it time, my boy," Dooley answered. "The gold is out there; we just gotta find it. Keep the faith, Reginald. Keep the faith."

"Alright, Dooley. Do you have an extra blanket or two? Maybe I'll sleep right here tonight and head back down to my claim in the morning."

"Sure thing. Those claim jumpers destroyed some of my things, but the blankets were of no interest to them when they discovered I wasn't hiding any gold under them."

"Speaking of hiding the gold, how did you keep them from finding your hiding place?" Reginald asked.

Dooley smiled, pulled off his boot, and passed it over to Bonesteel.

"Whew, what are you growing in there?" Bonesteel asked, turning his nose away from Dooley's boot.

"Oh, don't be a sissy. Go ahead, reach your hand down inside," Dooley said.

"No! Something might bite me," Bonesteel joked.

"Or you might find a heel full of gold," Dooley smiled.

"You're jesting," Bonesteel said. But he reached his hand down to the bottom of Dooley's boot. His fingers felt a small indentation that he used to slide the back of the heel forward in the boot, revealing a secret compartment in the heel of Dooley's boot. Beneath the slide, Bonesteel found a small pouch. He pulled it out and looked at it.

"Dooley! This is a lot of gold!"

"Sure is. And those boys would have never found it. Now hurry up, Reginald, and give me my boot back. My foot is getting cold."

THE NEXT DAY BONESTEEL returned to his claim with renewed hope of striking it rich. Just being around Dooley's optimistic attitude was an encouragement to Bonesteel. He set about the tedious task of panning for gold with renewed fervor.

For several hours Bonesteel knelt beside the stream, shaking the pan and looking for nuggets, digging his pan through the sand below the water, pulling up load after load of silt and sand. Most of what Bonesteel dug up was mud and rock, and then suddenly, he saw it! A piece of stone housing a small nugget of gold! "Whoooweee!" he shouted. "Dooley, you were right," he called to the old-timer even though he knew Corrigan was several miles upstream. Bonesteel grasped the stone so tightly it nearly cut his fingers. He raised it to his lips and kissed it. "Gold!" he said out loud. "I've actually found some gold."

Bonesteel tucked the nugget safely into a leather pouch in his pants pocket and then went back to work. A few minutes later he found another nugget!

He was so excited that he got up early the next morning and made the thirty-mile trek to Sacramento to register his claim at the mining office. He filed the claim and received a copy of the registration papers proving that the claim belonged to him. He carefully sealed the registration papers inside his coat.

As Bonesteel was filing his claim, two members of Buck English's band of claim jumpers stood off to the side of the registry office as though they were preparing papers to file their own claim. In actuality they were English's spies, sent to the office to check out anyone filing a new claim. They casually followed Reginald Bonesteel out of the office when he left and headed back to Grizzly Flats.

Later that afternoon the claim jumpers showed up at Bonesteel's tent. "You there," one of the men called out to Bonesteel as he panned for more gold. "Get out of the water. You've got ten minutes to pack your stuff and clear out. You're on our claim, and we intend to protect it."

Bonesteel looked up nonchalantly. "Oh, really?" he asked. "Pardon me, gentlemen. I didn't realize that this was your claim. I'll just be a minute, and we can clear this matter up right away." Bonesteel stepped out of the water, and in an unhurried manner, dried his hands and walked over to his tent, where he reached for Mr. Henry. He grabbed the rifle and fired two shots, purposely aiming above the heads of the two men on horseback. The horses reared, dumping both men into the cold stream behind them.

"I suggest that you be moving along now," Bonesteel said as he leveled his rifle at the two soaked claim jumpers. "Or my next shots will be much lower. This is my claim, and even though I haven't exactly struck it rich at this spot, I have a registered claim from the district mining office, and I will defend it to the death. So unless you men want to die, I suggest you go someplace else to dry off."

The two men, cold and wet, struggled to get back onto their horses and slowly moved off toward the trail behind the high pines along the river. When Bonesteel was certain they were gone, he went back to work, although he kept Mr. Henry close to the stream's edge.

Numerous men had found their fortunes along the riverbed, but Reginald Bonesteel was not one of them. Nevertheless, he felt sure that a thick vein of good was lying hidden close by, if he could only find it . . . He worked incessantly, sleeping in his tent set up right alongside his claim, rising each morning with the sun and working till the sun disappeared behind the hills each night. The only time he left his claim was to go into Grizzly Flats to get supplies and occasionally to check the telegram office to see if he had received any messages.

He had sent Elizabeth O'Banyon a brief telegram shortly after he settled in Grizzly Flats, just in case she or any of the Justice Riders needed to contact him. But he'd not heard from anyone since arriving in California.

Running out of supplies and patience, Reginald Bonesteel headed back to town. With him he carried his two lone gold nuggets. When he got to the bank in Grizzly Flats, he removed the nuggets from his leather pouch and looked at them. "I hate to cash in you two beauties, but I'm out of money so I really don't have much of a choice. Ah, but I believe there's much more good where you come from." He put the nuggets back in the pouch and placed the pouch on the counter in front of the bank teller's window.

"I'd like to exchange some gold for some cash," he said.

"Yes, sir. I'll be right with you," said a small, frail-looking man wearing a white shirt and black bow tie, with a leather apron over his clothes, as he stepped up to the other side of the teller's window. The man had a monocle-type magnifying glass strapped to his right eye, and he adjusted the magnifying power of the glass before examining Bonesteel's gold.

"Alright, sir. Let's see what you have there." He nodded toward Bonesteel's pouch.

Bonesteel dumped the two gold nuggets onto the counter and passed them over to the man with the magnifying glass.

"Hmm," the man said as he picked up one nugget and turned it from side to side under the monocle. "Mmm-hum," he said as he slowly moved the precious metal in his fingertips. "Very nice. And let's see the other one." He picked up the other chunk of gold and went through the same process. "Yes, yes, quite nice, sir. Please excuse me for a moment while I get your cash from the safe."

The man had been gone for less than a minute; then he returned with some money and began counting it out for Bonesteel. He counted a total of twenty one-dollar bills and handed them to Bonesteel.

"That's not exactly the fortune I was hoping for," Bonesteel said. "Are you sure that's all the stones are worth?"

"Oh, yes, sir. Quite sure," the banker replied. "The gold looks good, although not extremely deep in the stone. But what you have will be refined easily. Would you prefer to keep them until you have more?"

"No, thank you," Bonesteel said. "I actually need the cash now."

"Very well, sir. It is nice doing business with you." The banker picked up Bonesteel's gold and placed it in the bank safe.

"Yes, I hope to see you again soon," Bonesteel said, as he scooped up his money and started toward the door. He was about to go to the general store, when he thought, *I better go check the telegraph office before I head back up to the claim.*

Bonesteel didn't even go all the way in the telegraph office; he simply stuck his head in the door and asked the operator, "Any messages for Reginald Bonesteel?"

"Why, Mr. Bonesteel, please come in," a heavy-set man called to him from behind a desk near a fireplace with a blazing fire in the hearth. "I do believe something arrived for you just today. We were wondering how we might find you. Somebody said they thought you were working a claim out by Dooley Corrigan. Everyone in town knows Dooley. I was about to send a message to him in hopes that we might track you down."

Bonesteel stepped inside the warm office. "Well, in that case, I'm glad I came to town today."

"Yes, sir," the telegraph operator said. "Here you are; I have your telegram right here." The operator handed Bonesteel a single envelope.

Reginald Bonesteel tore open the yellow envelope and peeled opened the telegram. "Well, well," he said aloud more to himself than to the telegraph operator. "It's from Elizabeth." Standing beside the fireplace, he read the message from Elizabeth O'Banyon: "Remember O'Banyon. Ezra and Nate need help."

Bonesteel squeezed his forehead as he let out a low whistle. "I wonder what is so serious that Ezra Justice and Nathaniel York would need help."

"What's that, sir?" the telegraph operator asked. "Will you be responding to the message?"

"Yes, I will indeed." Bonesteel walked out of the telegraph office.

Outside, he stopped short. He reached inside his jacket and felt the claim registration notice still in his inside coat pocket. He'd brought the registration along just in case he needed to verify his right to the gold nuggets.

Bonesteel held up the claim registration documents proving his ownership of his claim. For a moment he thought of tearing the documents into a thousand little pieces, and then he thought of an old man who had helped him so much. He stepped back inside the telegraph office. "Would you do me a favor?" he asked.

"Why, sure, Mr. Bonesteel. How can I help you?" the telegraph operator said. "Would you like to send a telegram?"

"No, thanks. But would you see that Dooley Corrigan gets this claim registration next time he comes to town?" Bonesteel handed the official claim registration documents to the operator.

"I certainly will, Mr. Bonesteel. Any message you'd like to put with it."

"Yes; tell him I said thanks for everything."

"Thanks for everything. Anything else?"

"Tell him if he wants my tent or any of my panning materials or other belongings, he's welcome to them. I won't be needing them any more."

"I'll see that he gets that message, as well, Mr. Bonesteel."

Bonesteel gave the operator a few dollars for delivering the message and the claim registration to Dooley. Then Reginald Bonesteel stepped outside and took a deep breath of the fresh air. "So much for my fortune, I guess," he said.

Harry Whitecloud had noticed the attractive young woman in his medical school classroom during his first few weeks back at Princeton. He could tell that even though she was acting like a white person, the young woman was of Indian heritage.

One day during a break between classes, Harry saw the woman lying on the grass reading a book. He walked up to her and in a friendly manner said, "I can tell that you are an Indian. What tribe are you from?"

"I'm from the *white* tribe," the woman answered sarcastically.

"You may want to pretend you are a white woman, but by your features it is obvious that you are an Indian, and my guess is, that your ethnic background is the Sioux nation. Why are you dressing and acting like a white person, Miss . . . ah . . . ?"

"Serena Swiftson."

"And I'm Harry Whitecloud."

"Oh, yes. I know. Everyone on campus is talking about you. And in answer to your question, I act like a white person because I was raised by white parents."

Serena's tone softened as she told Harry a bit about her background. Serena was a Sioux, but her family had been killed during the westward expansion prior to the Civil War when she was just a child. An orphan, she had been rescued by white missionaries and had grown up with a wealthy white family in New York.

"Well, you know what it is like to grow up as a white person, but if you ever want to know what it is like growing up as an Indian on the Sioux nation, I'd be glad to tell you."

Harry turned and walked off to class.

Serena couldn't get Harry's probing comments out of her mind. *What would it be like if I hadn't been adopted? What would it have been like if my Indian parents had lived and I'd grown up in the tribe?*

One evening Harry was walking alone, which was normal because other Princeton students purposely avoided him. Serena approached Harry in a deserted area of campus.

"Hi, Serena. Fancy meeting you on the busiest part of campus," Harry said facetiously.

"That's not funny, Harry," Serena said with snip in her voice.

"It wasn't meant to be funny," Harry answered. "Why are you so afraid to let anyone know you are an Indian or even to be seen with an Indian?"

"You should know the answer to that without my having to tell you," Serena said sadly. "I want to belong, Harry, and I don't want to be looked at the way everybody else on this campus is looking at you!"

Serena Swiftson flicked her long dark hair out of her eyes and over her shoulder. "They are never going to accept you here, Harry."

"Serena, I'm not here for friendship; I'm here for learning."

"But Harry, you have to learn to get along!" Serena placed her hands on her slim hips and stood square with Harry as though challenging the tall, strong Whitecloud to a duel. "Look at you, Harry," Serena said. "Do you see any other men around here with hair halfway down their backs and wearing knee-high calfskin boots? You're an outcast, Harry!" Serena softened her tone a bit and stepped forward.

"If you'd cut your hair and dress more like the rest of the students, maybe they would accept you as an Indian."

"Like they have accepted you, Serena?" Harry could tell that his words stung the young woman, so he tried to explain. "Serena, you were raised as a white woman. You dress and act like everyone else on this campus."

"I don't go around telling everyone I'm an Indian, if that's what you mean. Why don't you want to blend in? Why do you want to make an issue of your background? It would be so much easier for you if you would just dress like everyone else here. Why do you want to make it harder than it already is?"

"Because I'm proud to be an Indian. Serena, you were never raised in a tribe. You don't really understand our culture.

We are a proud people. And I am proud to show who I am. I'm just sorry that you feel you have to hide your heritage.

"If the students can't accept you for who you are, then they are not your true friends anyway.

"One thing I learned during the war by watching two of my close friends, Ezra Justice and Nathaniel York, is that love and respect are earned, not given, and it goes a lot deeper than skin color.

"You may want to blend in and pretend that you are a white woman, and your parents are rich enough that the students, faculty, and administration of this university will treat you like a white woman. But I was raised as an Indian, and I don't want to pretend to be something I'm not. If they can't accept me for who I am, then I don't belong here."

Harry walked off, leaving Serena to think about his words.

Over the next few weeks, Harry and Serena frequently glanced at each other in class. They had a natural attraction for each other, but their differences regarding the way they dealt with their ethnic backgrounds kept them at bay. Harry realized that until Serena overcame her fear about what the other students thought of her, they could never have a close friendship.

One day as Harry was leaving class, Serena walked up to him in the hallway, in plain view of everybody. "Harry, I have to talk to you."

Harry looked around and noticed all the other students in the hallway. "Aren't you afraid of what everyone will think?"

"Never mind that," Serena said. "I heard Professor Reid's son, who happens to be in our class as well, talking to some of his friends. He told them that they have to make an example of you. He told them, 'If we let Indians come to this university, the next thing will be Negroes trying to enroll.' Harry, you have to be careful."

"Don't worry, Serena. I have survived four years of the war; I think I can survive some college students."

SERENA'S WARNINGS WERE NOT without reason. The town of Princeton boasted an eclectic population but few Indians. Slowly but surely the mood among most eastern communities and their government officials was leaning toward confining the Indian populations to reservations, especially now that gold had been discovered out west and more easterners were moving beyond the Mississippi River. At first, the Christians at Princeton and Harvard and other religious schools concerned themselves with preparing missionaries to convert the Indians to Christianity. More recently, though, somewhere between the 1830s and the end of the Civil War, the attitude became one of containment. Keep the Indians in their place, any place, just not my place.

Everywhere Whitecloud went, people stared at him as some sort of anomaly. So too, the hostility toward him on campus was nearly palpable. Even some of Harry's professors seemed less than enthusiastic about teaching him.

Professor Theodore Reid was especially hypocritical. While preaching to his students about the need to educate indigenous doctors from the Indian people to the Indian culture, he continually uttered verbal digs toward Whitecloud. "You're never going to get this material, are you?" he asked loudly in front of Harry's fellow students. "You Indians are just like the Negroes, strong of body but weak of mind."

"I beg your pardon, sir?" Whitecloud responded.

"You are just like the darkies," Professor Reid snarled, "just a little bit lighter."

"Excuse me, Professor," Whitecloud bristled, "but I thought this was an institution of higher learning, not a bastion of ignorance and prejudice."

"Class dismissed," Professor Reid announced abruptly.

The classroom quickly emptied as Whitecloud gathered his books and materials. *I might as well go to the library and get a real education by reading some good books*, Harry thought. Although it was only late afternoon, the sky had already darkened, and the autumn air was crisp as Harry started across campus, his feet swishing through the freshly fallen leaves. He passed the famous Princeton bell tower and headed toward the library. Just on the other side of the tower, as he crossed through an oak grove, six young men accosted him. "Hey, Injun, what makes you think you can act like a white man?" one of them challenged.

"Injun?" Harry repeated. He hadn't heard that word in quite a while. For the past few years during the war, his men had always respectfully referred to him as Sergeant Whitecloud. And then he had teamed up with Ezra and the Justice Riders. Although the men often called one another by their first names—except for Captain Justice, of course—no terms of derision were ever tolerated. But now, here he was trying to get his education at one of America's premier universities, so he could return to his people and help raise the standard of living, and these young punks were calling him "Injun." It was almost laughable.

But the six young men in front of him weren't laughing. They had spread out across the path, blocking Harry's way. "Which one of us do you want to take on first, Injun?" asked a large, tough-looking fellow standing in the middle of the path.

"You don't want to do that," Harry said calmly.

"What's the matter, Injun? Are you afraid? I heard you redskins weren't afraid of anything."

"I'd appreciate it if you would move out of my way," Harry said firmly.

"Come on, Injun. I have a better idea," one of the young men said. "How about a little duel?" The fellow pulled a pistol out of his pocket.

"Put the gun back in your pocket, kid," Harry said.

"Oh, I'll put it back in my pocket, but the next time I pull it out, it's going to be pointed at you. Now, I won't kill you; I'll just shoot you in the leg to let you know that we mean business around here. So reach your hand in your bag of tricks, and pull out whatever weapon you have, when my friend here says go."

"Kid, you're making a big mistake," Harry said.

"No, you made a mistake, Injun, coming to this university."

The young man put the gun in his pocket and turned toward his friend. "Edward, you say when."

Harry's hand was in his bag, but he kept his eye on the antagonist.

Edward was reluctant to give the word. The young man with the gun in his pocket said to Edward, "If you're too chicken to say it, then I will." He looked toward Harry, and shouted, "Go!"

The young man reached into his pocket, grabbing the handle of his pistol, but that's as far as he got.

With catlike instincts, Harry pulled his bowie knife out of his bag and threw the knife at the pocket the young man's gun was in. The blade sliced through his pants pocket and through the area just above his forefinger and middle finger, and lodged in his thigh. The young man screamed in pain while his friends stood watching in shock.

Harry walked over to the young man, whose hand was still stuck inside his pocket, his fingers wrapped around the pistol handle. Harry looked him in the eyes as he reached down and pulled his knife out of the punk's hand and thigh, blood oozing down his pants. The college student squealed in pain like a wild pig.

"I warned you," Harry said as he wiped the bowie's blade on the punk's shirt. "Now you boys get him to the doctor before he bleeds to death."

THE NEXT MORNING, as Harry was walking to class, Serena came running up to him. "Word is out all over campus about what happened last night. Are you crazy?" she asked grabbing Harry's arm. "Are you trying to give them a reason to kill you?"

"They tried last night, Serena. They were just a bunch of punks. It was nothing."

"Nothing? Do you realize that you stabbed Professor Reid's son?"

"Reid? So that's who the loudmouth was, huh?"

"Professor Reid is in the process of filing assault charges against you. Oh, Harry, don't you see? Don't you understand? They are just looking for an excuse to get rid of you, and you played right into their hands!"

"I didn't kill him."

"Oh, well, that's progress!"

"I have to get to class," Harry said. "But I want to take a walk first and think about this."

"Well, I'll walk with you."

"Serena, if you are seen walking with me, things could be different for you here. You'll really find out who your friends are."

"I can deal with that," Serena said with fire in her eyes.

Harry looked at her and smiled. "Better be careful, Serena; the Indian in you is coming out!"

"Yeah, I never realized I was so hot-blooded," Serena said with a laugh.

"On the way I want to stop by the telegraph office," Harry said. The two walked together all the way across campus toward the telegraph office. As they walked, Harry told Serena stories from his youth growing up on the Sioux nation.

At the Western Union office, Harry walked up to the operator and said, "My name is Harry Whitecloud. Is there a telegram for me?

The operator looked through the stack of incoming telegrams and pulled one out. "Yes, you do have one," he said, handing the telegram to Harry.

Harry opened the Western Union envelope and read it while Serena looked on. A look of concern flashed across Harry's face.

"Is anything wrong, Harry?" Serena asked.

"Remember O'Banyon," Harry read aloud. "Ezra and Nate need you. Signed, Elizabeth."

"Elizabeth? Who is Elizabeth?" Serena wanted to know. "An old girlfriend? Who are Ezra and Nate? And what's an O'Banyon?"

"Serena, my friends need my help, so I'll be leaving immediately."

"Leaving? Where are you going? Harry! Go where?"

"To Tennessee. My friends are in trouble."

"Harry! When are you coming back?"

Harry looked into Serena's eyes. "Truthfully, Serena, I'm not sure what I'll be doing. I'll figure that out after I help my friends. Serena, you're going to be a doctor, and the Sioux nation could sure use your help. I'd like for you to think about that after you graduate."

"I don't know, Harry. But I promise you, I will think about it."

Will you young ladies please hurry? We're going to be late for church if you don't stop primping and start moving," Pastor Octavius Bennett called to his daughters. "And besides, Carlos and Roberto are not coming to see you; they are coming to worship the Lord."

"We know that, Papa," Sara called from the bedroom. "We just want you to be proud of us. And yes, of course, it will be nice to see Carlos and Roberto at church."

Pastor Bennett smiled and cringed slightly at the same time. He knew full well that Carlos and Roberto's interest was not so much in spiritual matters or even in his daughters. The two members of the Justice Riders were concerned that Pastor Bennett had received death threats since moving to St. Louis. The pastor had been emphasizing in his sermons that the gospel was for all people, regardless of their skin color, and therefore the church should be open to all people, regardless of their race. Not everybody in St. Louis saw things that way, however.

Especially since the end of the war, when so many freed slaves were packing onto steamboats, coming up the Mississippi River, and migrating to the St. Louis area.

In fact, a number of people in Pastor Bennett's own congregation adamantly opposed encouraging people of various races to worship together. They let their sentiments be known to Pastor Bennett in no uncertain terms shortly after his arrival at the church.

Simon Shortridge, the chairman of the church board of directors, comprised of some of the leading citizens of St. Louis, confronted Pastor Bennett after a Sunday service within weeks of the new pastor's arrival. The chairman spoke quietly but virulently. "We'd never have brought you here if we had thought your intentions were to try to integrate our church."

"I thought you brought me here to preach the gospel, Mr. Shortridge," Pastor Bennett said calmly. "And I'm sure you recall that the angels announced the Savior's birth to a group of shepherds keeping watch over their flock out in the fields." Pastor Bennett paused, as though waiting for Shortridge to fill in the rest of the story. Shortridge remained silent, simply glaring at Bennett, so the pastor continued.

"The angel said, 'Don't be afraid, for I'm bringing you good news of great joy . . . for *all people*," the pastor emphasized. "'For in the city of David there has been born to you a Savior who is Christ the Lord.' I'm sure you recall the Christmas story, do you not, Mr. Shortridge? And how about the Great Commission Jesus gave to us after he died and rose again?

Do you remember that he commanded us to go into all the world and make disciples of all nations?"

"Don't toy with me, Preacher," Simon Shortridge growled.

"Oh, I'm not trifling with you, Mr. Shortridge. But do you realize that even in the book of Revelation, when the Bible talks about who is going to be in heaven, the Word says that there will be people there from every tribe and tongue and nation? If we are going to be together in heaven, why can't we worship together in our church now?"

"Listen, Preacher," Simon Shortridge's face reddened as he spoke. "I've lived in this town all my life. And I'm telling you that our people are not ready to hear that kind of message." Simon took a breath, trying to calm himself. "It's not that we have anything against those people—the darkies or the Indians—but they have their own way of living and believing, and we have ours, so let's keep it that way. That's all I'm saying."

Pastor Bennett's voice softened a bit. "Mr. Shortridge, I feel strongly that we should open the church to everyone, regardless of color. Because there are so many Indian tribes nearby and because so many freed slaves are moving to St. Louis, I was hoping this would be a perfect place to open the doors to all races."

"Pastor, they are not going to come," Shortridge insisted. "Trust me, I've lived here. And I believe your noble intentions will reap a harvest of dangerous results."

THE FOLLOWING WEEK Pastor Bennett once again preached a sermon in which he encouraged racial harmony. Although the pastor didn't know it, one of the people in the congregation that morning was Edwin Dark, a reporter for the *St. Louis Dispatch.*

After the service Dark stopped to talk with Pastor Bennett when he was shaking hands with people leaving the sanctuary. "Are you serious about this new message of racial reconciliation?" the reporter asked.

Pastor Bennett smiled kindly. "Well, sir, it is not really a new message at all. It has been with us since the time of Christ. The family of God is made up of people from every ethnic and economic background. Our faith in Jesus unites us; it should not divide us."

"That sounds real nice," Edwin Dark said, shaking Pastor Bennett's hand, "but I am certain your idealistic notions are totally unrealistic and will never work."

As soon as Edwin Dark left the church, he went straight to the newspaper office and began writing an article about how Pastor Bennett wanted the churches of St. Louis to become racially integrated. The following week Dark's article hit the press, and news spread quickly about the new preacher who had come to St. Louis with thoughts of integrating the various communities.

Simon Shortridge was outraged when he read Dark's article, as were the other church elders. Several suggested firing Pastor Bennett on the spot.

The day after the *Dispatch* article hit the streets, Pastor Bennett was walking toward the church when three men in their late twenties or early thirties fell in step with him, one on each side of him and one man behind the preacher. The men purposely began bumping into the pastor as he walked, jostling him from side to side, stepping in front of him, cursing him, calling him names, and trapping him between them.

At first Pastor Bennett tried to ignore their belligerent words and actions, but appeasing them only encouraged more outrageous behavior and language. Pastor Bennett stopped on the boardwalk. "Can I help you gentlemen?"

"You sure can, preacher man. You can stop telling people to bring the darkies to your church. We don't want no Redskins in church, either. You've got no right messing with our town like that."

"Oh, really? I don't believe I've seen you men in any of our recent church services, now have I?" Pastor Bennett asked.

"Ain't none of your business, Preacher, where we go to church, or if we go to church at all. But it is *our* business when you start telling your congregation to bring people with black skin and red skin into the same room with people of white skin."

"Oh, I see," Pastor Bennett said, as he began walking toward the church again. The three men continued harassing the pastor, cursing and threatening him. "Look, you darkie lover, if you keep encouraging that sort of thing, you're gonna get hurt—bad! Do you understand?"

"Oh, we understand perfectly well," said Roberto Hawkins. He and Carlos had just stepped out of the hotel where they were staying and were walking down the street toward

Pastor Bennett when they saw the three men bothering him and heard their cursing. They hurried up to Pastor Bennett and blocked the boardwalk after he had passed by, standing face-to-face with the three ruffians.

"Come on, boys," Pastor Bennett said, "I really need your help at the church."

"We'll be right there, Reverend Bennett," Carlos called. "Just as soon as we clean some rubbish off the street."

"Carlos!" Pastor Bennett called. "Please don't do anything foolish."

But Pastor Bennett's words were too late. Carlos's lightning fast left hook had already connected with one man's face. Carlos came back with a strong right-hand punch to the chin that sent the man tumbling to the ground.

Meanwhile Roberto had launched a powerful right hook toward the man on his left, knocking him over the boardwalk railing and into the street. Roberto turned, reared back, and threw another strong right at the man closest to the wall of the building. Roberto's punch caught the man high, as Carlos simultaneously blasted a blow into the man's stomach. The tough-looking ruffian doubled over, crumpling onto the boardwalk.

"See you boys in church on Sunday," Carlos said. Then he and Roberto hurried to catch up with Pastor Bennett.

Following that encounter, the Hawkins twins began attending church services with the Bennetts every time the church doors were open. The twins hadn't given up on their hopes of going to New Orleans, but just about the time they'd think things were settled enough at the church that they could take off, something else would happen, giving them some reason to stay a little longer to help.

Tensions continued to build among the church members themselves over Pastor Bennett's messages about bringing in people of various races. "It is hard to disagree with what the pastor is saying," Martha McConnell, one of the leading women of the congregation, told a group of women, "but we just don't want those kind of people attending our church. They have their own churches. Let them worship God there."

Pastor Bennett continued to encourage Negroes and Indians to attend the church, but none ever did. One night after a particularly difficult service, Octavius Bennett said to his wife Mildred and their daughters, "If I can't get them to come to our church, I'll take the message to them."

"What do you mean, Papa?" Mary asked.

"I mean that I am going to go preach the good news about God's love in the poorest parts of town," Pastor Bennett said. "I'm going to tell them that God loves them regardless of what color their skin, and people everywhere who really want to know God must come to him through a relationship with Jesus Christ. There's no other way."

"Won't that be dangerous?" Mary asked. "Are you sure it is safe for you to go into that part of town?"

"Oh, it shouldn't be too bad," Pastor Bennett replied. "After all, I'm sure your friends Carlos and Roberto will want to go along with me since they seem to insist on serving as my personal bodyguards."

"*Our* friends, Papa," Sara said.

"Yes, that's what I said, your friends."

"But Carlos and Roberto are not merely friends to Mary, Ruth, and me; they are friends to all of us."

"Yes, of course they are, dear," Pastor Bennett said. "Some of us are just closer friends than others." He looked at Mary and smiled. "Isn't that right, Mary?"

Mary looked back at her father and blushed. "Oh, Papa, stop teasing me. Carlos and I are just friends."

"Friends," Pastor Bennett repeated.

"Yes, Father," Mary said emphatically. "Friends. I wish it were more, but Carlos refuses to consider a serious relationship right now."

"You sure like sitting next to him during church services," Ruth piped up.

"That's simply so I can help Carlos understand the service better," Mary said.

"Oh! He must not understand much," Ruth teased, "because you sure seem to be sitting mighty close during the services."

"Yes, well, at any rate, I am going to go to the poorest sections of town to tell the people about Jesus," Pastor Bennett continued. "I'm going to tell them that God is color-blind. He doesn't care about the color of a person's skin. If I can't say it here in the church, I'll say it out there in the streets."

Mildred Bennett pensively folded her hands in her lap. "Please, Octavius. I know you will do what you feel in your heart that you must, but please, I beg of you, reconsider this course of action."

"Mildred, don't try to talk me out of this," Pastor Bennett replied. "I am determined to bring these people together. Now that the Negroes are no longer slaves, they should be treated equally in the schools, in the community, and especially in the churches."

"I know, I know," Mildred said, covering her face with her hands so Octavius would not see her tears. "But why do you have to be the person to lead the way? Why not let someone from this community get things started, and then you can assist the work?"

"I'm doing what I feel God wants me to do, Mildred," Pastor Bennett said. "I don't know if this is the best way to go about it or not, but I will try. The Lord knows my heart; he knows my motives. If my methods are wrong, I'm open to changing my course of actions. But right now I feel compelled to take the gospel into the darkest parts of our city."

"OK, Octavius," Mildred said, as she hugged her husband and kissed him lightly. "I will pray for you every moment that you are gone."

WHEN PASTOR BENNETT told Carlos and Roberto about his new plans to start going into the poorest sections of town to preach the gospel, they were concerned. "You will definitely need us there," Roberto said.

"That's for sure," Carlos agreed. "I guess we'll have to hold off on New Orleans."

For the next several weeks, Pastor Bennett preached in the church on Sunday morning and evening to an all-white congregation. Then during the week he and the Hawkins twins went to the poorest parts of town, preaching to the poor and downtrodden. Usually the pastor simply struck up conversations with one or two men around a campfire, and before long a small crowd would gather to hear what the white preacher had to say. Most of the people who listened to Pastor Bennett were former slaves. "I want you to know that our church is always open to you," he told his predominantly black audiences, as he shared a message of love.

"You can come down here and tell us about how welcome we are, Reverend," one extremely thin, almost gaunt Negro man lamented, "but it just ain't true."

"What do you mean, sir?" Pastor Bennett asked.

"Those people don't want us there, and those good church folk would just as soon kill a darkie for even wantin' to sit down inside their church buildings," the black man replied.

"I beg to disagree with you, sir," Bennett protested, "and I am sorely sorry if you have experienced bad manners at the hands of supposedly Christian people, but please don't blame God for the ungodly words, actions, or attitudes of some who merely use his name and don't live as he says."

"Tell that to your own people," the Negro man said. "We see it; you white folks don't."

Day after day Pastor Bennett and the Hawkins twins traveled several miles across town to some of the poorest neighborhoods in St. Louis. On several occasions, along the way the twins had to defend the pastor from the venomous insults and threats from some of the white people who knew that he was trying to "mix up the community," as they put it.

After a while even Carlos and Roberto began to doubt the wisdom of Pastor Bennett's efforts. "Why are you doing this, Pastor Bennett?" Roberto asked. "It is obvious that the various racial groups in this town don't want anything to do with one another. Why try to force the issue?"

"Good question," Carlos chimed in. "After all, you can't make people love one another."

"You may be right, boys, but I feel I have to try," Pastor Bennett replied.

Carlos and Roberto simply shook their heads. "As long as you're trying, there's going to be trouble," said Carlos.

Although the Hawkins twins sometimes argued with the pastor, they still respected him and wanted to protect him, even though they were growing more and more eager to get on their way to New Orleans.

One Sunday, after another particularly painful confrontation between Pastor Bennett and a hostile group of parishioners, Carlos looked at Roberto and said, "They're just not ready to start embracing one another."

"I know what you mean," Roberto replied. "God forbid, if we left, and Pastor Bennett and his family were killed, we'd have a hard time living with ourselves."

"Well, I just hope they come to their senses before we're too old to have any fun!" Carlos said. "I want to get to New Orleans while we are still young enough to enjoy it. Bonesteel has probably already struck it rich in California, and here we are stuck in St. Louis."

PASTOR BENNETT'S MESSAGE of love and reconciliation continued to fall on deaf ears, rejected by the members of his congregation as well as the people in the poor communities to which he tried to bring hope.

Discouraged and nearly ready to quit the ministry, Pastor Bennett sat down on a log near a campfire in the inner section of the city. Carlos and Roberto hovered nearby, but they could tell that the pastor needed some time to think or pray by himself. "Let's leave him alone," Roberto said to Carlos. "We can keep an eye on everything from over here." He nodded toward a makeshift bench made from a tree that had been cut down and placed over two large rocks. The twins sat down and waited for Pastor Bennett.

Octavius Bennett opened his Bible to about the center and placed it on the log next to him. He put his hands over his face and prayed, "God, I sure could use some answers here. I've been trying to do the right thing, but it just doesn't seem to be working. Please give me the insight I need to do what you want me to do."

A slight breeze rustled the pages of Pastor Bennett's Bible and caught his attention. He picked up the Bible and looked at the page. The wind had blown the pages open to an Old Testament passage, Ecclesiastes 3. Pastor Bennett held the Bible in front of him and read the first few verses of the chapter:

To everything there is a season, and a time to every purpose under the heaven: A time to be born, and a time to die; a time to plant, and a time to pluck up that which is planted; a time to kill, and a time to heal; a time to break down, and a time to build up.

Pastor Bennett mulled over the words; he had read the passage numerous times before and had quoted it often at funerals, but for some reason the words struck him with new meaning. "To everything there is a season, and a time . . ."

Just then an elderly Negro came over and sat next to Pastor Bennett. "Good evenin', sir," he said. "Mind if I sit a spell with you?"

"No, of course not," Pastor Bennett said. "Be my guest." He nodded toward a spot on the log.

"Gabriel's the name, sir. Gabriel Michaels, pastor of the First Church of God up the way here." The Negro reached out his hand toward Pastor Bennett, and the two men shook hands. Even in the semi-darkness, Octavius Bennett could not help noticing the stark contrast between Gabriel Michaels' dark hand and that of his own white hand.

"I'm glad to meet you, Pastor Michaels," Octavius said. "I didn't know there was a church in this part of town."

"Oh, yes, we have been at work in this town for a lot of years now," the elderly black man said. "And I want you to know that I appreciate what you have been trying to do— pulling black and white folk together and all. And working to reach the Indians, too.

"But I gotta tell you something that you ain't gonna want to hear."

Pastor Bennett looked at the man quizzically. "What would that be, sir?"

Pastor Michaels continued, "You're not going to like it, but it's the truth, and I've been sent here to tell it to you."

"Sent by whom?" Pastor Bennett asked.

"That part isn't any of your concern right now," the elderly Negro said, looking Bennett in the eyes. "But you do need to know that you are right. God does want people from every tribe, tongue, and nation to be able to worship together. But, my brother, it is too early for the message of reconciliation to take hold in men and women's hearts just yet. With the war just ending and the slaves only recently receiving their freedom, there's still a lot of hatred in the air between the North and South, as well as white folk and black folk. Repentance is the order of the day right now. Repentance always precedes revival, which leads to restoration and reconciliation. Pardon my alliteration, but once I get going, my preacher mode takes over," Pastor Michaels smiled, "but you know what I mean.

"Whites always felt that blacks were subservient and should be treated that way. Blacks allowed bitterness to cause them to become calloused on the inside. Neither of those attitudes pleases God, and both must be forgiven. Only with time and with God's help will people change. What you are praying for will happen one day, but it is going to take some time. And the timing is important. The secret to having the peace of God in your heart is to accept his timetable."

"And what do I do in the meantime?" Pastor Bennett asked.

"Pastor, you just keep telling 'em about Jesus and how he can change their hearts. I'm sure you remember that Jesus said, 'If I be lifted up, I will draw all men unto me.'"

Pastor Bennett nodded his head. He knew that the wise old black pastor was reminding him of an important truth: only God can change a person's heart. Pastor Bennett realized that he'd been trying to do God's work on his own timetable, under his own power, rather than God's. Even though his intentions regarding racial reconciliation were noble, it wasn't the right time; nor was it the right way of going about it. Bennett dropped to his knees. "Oh, God, please forgive me for trying to do things my way rather than yours," Pastor Bennett prayed. "You know my heart, that I've only wanted to bring people together through your love. I surrender, Lord, and from now on I will trust you with this matter."

For more than a minute the two men of God sat quietly in front of the fire. Pastor Bennett had come to the realization that integration had to be on God's timetable rather than his, for only God can make people's hearts tender enough that they will want to live together in peace.

Still contemplating this truth, Pastor Bennett became aware of Pastor Michaels's voice. "People have to learn to look beyond the color of skin," Pastor Michaels was saying, "but instead, look to the Spirit. They won't do it unless encouraged by someone. That's where you and I come in. It's our job to help people see things from God's perspective. When people see one another in the Spirit, they won't worry about the color of a person's skin."

"You are so right," Pastor Bennett said. "Hold on, here, one moment, Pastor Michaels. I'd like my friends to hear your perspective." Pastor Bennett got up to walk over to where Carlos and Roberto were sitting. "Hey, fellows; come over here," Pastor Bennett called. "I want you to meet someone."

Carlos and Roberto hurried over to Pastor Bennett.

"I want you to meet Reverend Gabriel Michaels, pastor of the First Church of God," he said, turning to look at Pastor Michaels. But when Pastor Bennett turned around to introduce his new friend, the elderly Negro pastor was gone.

"Pastor, we've been watching you. There's been no one else here," Carlos said. "In fact, we almost came running over when you dropped to your knees. Then we realized that you were praying."

"But I don't understand! He was right there by the fire a few seconds ago," Pastor Bennett replied. Suddenly a look of understanding dawned on Pastor Bennett's face. He took a deep breath and said, "Well, boys, I think I was visited by an angel."

"An angel?" Carlos gushed. "Are you sure?"

"Well, angels are messengers sent from God, and he sure was a messenger from God to me," Pastor Bennett said. "Let's go home and see if we can convince Mrs. Bennett to make us one of her special dinners to celebrate our freedom—freedom for all the slaves but also freedom from the slavery of having to do things my way."

"Sounds like a good reason to celebrate to me," Carlos quipped.

Pastor Bennett put one arm around Carlos's shoulder and the other around Roberto's. "We know, Carlos," he said with a smile. "Almost anything is a good reason for you to celebrate. But this is a really good one."

WITH TENSIONS EASING AT THE CHURCH, Carlos and Roberto felt it was time for them to move on to New Orleans. A few days before they packed up to leave, the twins decided to go out for a night on the town in St. Louis. Although they had received a sizable sum of money from General Sherman, the Hawkins brothers had spent more than half of their funds helping Pastor Bennett.

"We have about eight hundred dollars between us," Roberto said, counting out their money on a bed in their hotel room. "Let's go find a good gambling spot where we can run this eight hundred dollars up to two thousand before we go to New Orleans."

"Or maybe even three thousand!" Carlos agreed.

The Hawkins twins went out gambling that night, but nearly everything they tried fell apart. For two extremely adept card sharks like the twins, their losing streak was even more frustrating. "I think we've heard too many sermons from

Pastor Bennett," Roberto said, "about all those evil vices associated with gambling."

"Maybe so," Carlos said. "All that talk about being a good steward of what God has given you is messing up my game!"

By the time the twins got back to their hotel that night, instead of two or three thousand dollars, they had little more than six hundred dollars between the two of them. Carlos shook his head as he plopped down on the bed and pulled off his boots. "All I know is, that was the worst streak of luck we've ever had in our lives!"

Roberto nodded. "You are right, Carlos. What happened? We played just like we always do, but nothing seemed to work. It was almost as if the deck was stacked against us."

"Well, let's go to New Orleans anyway," Carlos said, "and hopefully our luck will change there."

MILDRED BENNETT COOKED UP a delicious meal as a going away present for Carlos and Roberto the night before their departure. It was a bittersweet time for everyone around the table, as Pastor and Mrs. Bennett had come to regard Carlos and Roberto as their own sons. Of course, the girls were delighted that Carlos and Roberto could come for dinner but deeply saddened at the knowledge that the twins were leaving St. Louis.

"It just won't be the same around here without you two," Sara gushed.

"No, it won't," said Mary, looking into Carlos's eyes.

"When will you be coming back?" Ruth asked.

"Oh, I don't know," Roberto said with grin, as he swallowed a big spoonful of mashed potatoes. "But I have a feeling that you haven't seen the last of us."

"I certainly hope not," Mary said, her eyes never leaving Carlos's.

"We sure have appreciated you men staying nearby during the difficult honeymoon period for us here in St. Louis," Pastor Bennett said. "On more than a few occasions, I thought we might all be tarred and feathered, or worse, but I think we are through the worst of things now."

"Yes, thank you so much for standing with Octavius," Mrs. Bennett said. She put her hand up to her face, shielding her words from her husband but speaking so Carlos and Roberto could see. "And for protecting him," she mouthed the words.

"You are quite welcome, ma'am," Roberto said. "We've enjoyed our time in St. Louis. It was . . . er . . . ahh, different from what we expected, but we have had a good time here. We will miss all of you." He turned to Ruth, the youngest, who was seated next to him. "Especially you, dear Ruth!" Roberto threw his arm around Ruth's shoulder and hugged her to his side.

Ruth squealed in delight. "We'll miss you, too, Roberto. And you, too, Carlos. Won't we, Mary?"

"Yes, we will," Mary said softly. "Mother, may I be excused from the dishwashing chores tonight? I'd like to speak to Carlos privately for a few minutes before he and Roberto must go."

"Certainly, dear," Mildred said, with a twinkle in her eye. "I think we can manage without you tonight."

"May I speak with you on the front porch, Carlos?" Mary asked.

Carlos looked to Pastor Bennett as though asking his permission. "Yes, that will be fine," Pastor Bennett said.

Mary led Carlos onto the front porch while the other girls busied themselves clearing the table. Pastor Bennett, Mildred, and Roberto sat down to talk in the living room.

Outside, Mary mustered her courage to ask Carlos the question that had been burning in her heart for weeks now. "Carlos, do you . . ." She paused, searching for just the right words. "Carlos, do you fancy me at all?" she finally blurted. "I don't mean just as a friend, or as the pastor's daughter, but you know. Do you *like* me?"

"Of course I like you, Mary," Carlos said softly. "You are a wonderful, beautiful, intelligent young woman, and I am proud to have you as my friend."

"Your friend?" Mary asked.

"Yes, my friend," Carlos repeated. "You have been a great friend to me since the day we met."

"Forgive me for speaking so bluntly, Carlos, but we haven't much time. Do you think we might ever be more than mere *friends*?" Mary blushed in the twilight, feeling as though she might have spoken too much too soon. She hurriedly continued before Carlos could respond. "I know I'm younger than you are, but I am rapidly approaching a marriageable age, and well . . . you must know that my heart has been drawn toward yours . . ."

"Mary, Mary," Carlos gently interrupted her, reaching out and placing his hands on her shoulders. "Slow down. Take it easy. Yes, I do fancy you; in fact, I like you a lot."

Carlos awkwardly dropped his hands to his sides and continued. "But Mary, I'm not ready to settle down. If I were ready to be married, it would be with someone like you. Right now Roberto and I have some things that we want to do. We'll never be settled until we do them. But when that day comes, I want a wife just like you."

Tears trickled from Mary's eyes, and she said, "But you're leaving, Carlos. I may never see you again."

"Yes, we are leaving first thing in the morning, but don't worry. If God wants us together, nothing will be able to keep us apart."

"God? Do you think . . . ?"

"Sure, haven't you and your family been teaching me how to trust God for everything? And doesn't the Good Book say that a good wife is from the Lord?"

"Yes, but I wasn't sure you believed that strongly, Carlos," Mary said.

"Oh, I believe, Mary," Carlos said. "I've seen too much over these past few years not to believe."

"Then what about us?" Mary asked.

"You told me one time, Mary, that you wanted to go to college to become a nurse. I think you should pursue that goal."

"Really?"

Carlos continued to encourage her, "Yes, of course, Mary; fulfill your God-given destiny. Don't let anyone tell you that you can't do it. Get your nursing degree and become the best nurse ever."

"And what about us, Carlos?"

"Us?"

"You and me, together some day?"

"Well, if that happens, then I'll be married to the prettiest nurse in the new territories," Carlos said with a smile. "But let's not get ahead of ourselves." Carlos pulled Mary close to him and held her for a moment. "We better get in now, before you catch your death of cold. Nurses have to be healthy, you know." Carlos released Mary and opened the door for her as they stepped back inside the house, both of their faces a bit flushed with color, and both of their hearts slightly broken.

Before the twins left the Bennett family that night, Pastor Bennett prayed a heartfelt prayer over them, asking God to bless and protect Carlos and Roberto, to help them stand up for what is right and to bring them all back together again sometime if it were part of God's plan.

"Amen!" Mary said loudly, causing the others in the room to chuckle.

"And God, please give Mary patience," Pastor Bennett prayed. "Amen!"

Carlos and Roberto went to each family member, thanking them for their kindness, when suddenly Carlos stopped and said, "Pastor and Mrs. Bennett, Roberto and I have about six hundred dollars left of our mustering out pay from the army. We'd like to give it to you."

"We would?" Roberto nearly gasped.

"Yes," Carlos continued, "with the way our luck has been running recently, if we take that money to New Orleans, we'll probably lose it anyhow."

"We would?" Roberto whispered again.

"So instead of wasting the money, we'd like to do something good with it. I know that Mary would like to further her education, and maybe Sara and Ruth want to do the same. So to help each of the girls get started, Roberto and I would like to give you the six hundred dollars, two hundred dollars for each of the girls."

"You would?" the three Bennett girls said almost simultaneously.

Roberto smiled as he reached into his knapsack and retrieved the money. "Yes, we would," he said, handing a wad of cash to Pastor Bennett.

"Carlos, Roberto, I don't even know how to thank you," Pastor Bennett said. "I've been trying to save a little here and there for the girls' education, but there hasn't been much money left over for anything, much less saving for college. We will be forever grateful to you men."

"Oh, don't thank us too much," Carlos said with a laugh. "In our line of work, we tend to get a lot of scrapes, cuts, and bruises, so if your daughters become nurses, we might need their help once in a while." Carlos looked at Mary, whose face was beaming with joy.

Carlos and Roberto waved good-bye and returned to their hotel room. They were sad to leave their good friends but excited about setting out on a new adventure.

The following morning the twins were up at sunrise, packing up their meager belongings, preparing to leave for New Orleans. They went downstairs and stepped over to the counter to check out. The hotel manager, Frank Carlson, an elderly gentleman with glasses that rode on the edge of his nose, was working behind the counter when the twins stepped up to settle up their account. "We're going to be leaving you today, Mr. Carlson," Roberto told the man behind the front desk as he placed the large room key on the counter. "We've enjoyed staying with you, but it is time for us to head on down to New Orleans."

"Well, you boys have been good tenants," Mr. Carlson said, sliding his glasses back up his nose again. "We're going to miss seeing you around here. Let me pull out your account, and I'll have you on your way in a minute." Mr. Carlson fumbled with some papers in a file drawer and pushed his glasses back on his nose again. "Oh, wait a minute," he said. "I'm sure glad you boys stopped by this morning. Someone just brought this over from the telegraph office. It is addressed to Carlos or Roberto Hawkins. Since I can never tell you fellas apart, I'll just give it to either one of you." Mr. Carlson handed a telegram to Roberto.

"Thank you, Mr. Carlson," Roberto said. "We've appreciated your hospitality during our stay."

"What's it say?" Carlos asked, pointing at the telegram. "Hurry up, Roberto; open it up."

"I was thinking that we ought to stop by to send a telegram to Elizabeth O'Banyon, to let her know that we are heading to New Orleans," Roberto said as he tore open the envelope.

"The last note we sent to her was shortly after we arrived here at the hotel in St. Louis."

Roberto stared at the Western Union telegram. "Well, well, well, looks like Elizabeth has had some contact from Ezra and Nate."

"Really? What does it say?" Carlos looked over Roberto's shoulder and read out loud, "Remember O'Banyon. Ezra and Nate need you." The telegram was signed by Elizabeth O'Banyon.

"I guess we didn't need that gambling money after all," Roberto said.

"No, but it looks as though we're going to have some excitement, just the same," Carlos replied, rubbing his hands together. "How fast can we get to Tennessee?"

Ezra Justice gathered his workers and their family members in the carriage house. "I know you have suffered terribly at the hands of the Ku Klux Klan, but I want you to know that help is on the way. I can't tell you when it will get here, but it is coming. So be strong and courageous, and don't be afraid."

The workers nodded in agreement as a buzz of nervous excitement rippled through the group.

Ezra looked at Nate and said, "I need to talk to you for a minute. Let's step outside." The men walked out behind the carriage house. "Nate, I am riding over to Lewisburg to contact General Sherman to let him know what is going on here. I don't dare send this telegram from Pulaski because I'm sure the telegraph operator there is either afraid of the Klan or one of them. Either way, I don't want him giving away our secrets. I'll be back as soon as I can. In the meantime, these folks could sure use an encouraging sermon about now."

"You're right, Ezra," Nate said. "I'll do my best, with God's help." Nate returned to the carriage house to speak to the workers while Ezra mounted his horse and galloped off toward Lewisburg.

"Today is Thursday," Nate began his impromptu message. "And I'm thinking of another Thursday evening in the Bible when Jesus led his disciples into the garden of Gethsemane. He knew he was facing a tough road ahead in the next few days, so he knelt down and prayed. I mean he prayed hard, too, so intensely that the Scripture says he was sweating big drops like blood.

"Jesus didn't ask his heavenly Father for an easy way. He prayed, 'Father, if there is any other way but that cross out there, then let this cup pass from me; but if not, well, then let your will be done.'

"Now, friends, we don't know what these next few days are going to bring us, but we can be fairly sure that they are going to be rough. In the midst of this stressful time, I'm not praying that God will give us an easy way; I'm praying that God's will gets done."

"Amen," Sophia called out.

"Let God's will be done!" someone else shouted.

Nate smiled and continued. "One thing we can be sure of," he said. "God's will for us is good. When God's people were literally in bondage, the prophet Jeremiah reminded them that even in the face of tough times, God's plan for them was for good, not evil, to prosper them and to give them a hope and a good future."

"That's right!" one of the workers called.

"So no matter how difficult things get over the next few days, don't forget: God has a plan. And he is going to work things out for our good, no matter who tries to bring evil against us." Nate paused and rubbed his chin before he spoke again. "Now listen carefully; I'm not saying it is going to be easy."

The group of workers and their family members grew extremely quiet and somber, listening intently to Nate's words.

"Some of us might get hurt," Nate continued quietly. "Some of us might even die. But rest assured, we are going to do what is right, no matter what the cost."

The workers broke into a spontaneous chorus of amens, as they began to pray for God's blessing and that his will be done.

PRIOR TO EZRA'S LEAVING the property, three members of the KKK had been lurking nearby, spying on the plantation. When they saw Justice riding off by himself, they decided to take advantage of the opportunity to kill Ezra. "If we take Justice's body back to town strapped over his saddle, imagine how happy that will make the judge," one of the gunslingers said. The others nodded approvingly.

The three gunmen rode ahead of Ezra, looking for a place where they could best mount an ambush. They found a small knoll that looked perfect for what they had in mind. They prepared to bushwhack Ezra when he got within striking distance.

Riding along at a leisurely pace, Ezra was thinking about what had to be done, not just on the plantation but to rid the area of the Klan's influence. Justice knew all too well the debilitating effects fear can have on a community. He'd seen it almost all his life, growing up in a place where fear was regularly used to keep people in their places.

Ezra knew, too, that fear and an awareness of danger are not the same thing. As he rode along, Justice sensed impending danger nearby, but he was not afraid. He had good reason to be confident. All the skills that Ezra had acquired in the military over his years of service were still sharp. Men had tried to kill Ezra numerous times, but Ezra had an inbred instinct to feel danger.

Now, as he traveled along the trail toward Lewisburg, he sensed danger even before he saw it. His razor-sharp instincts were on high alert. Just as Ezra cantered near the knoll where the men were preparing to ambush him, he noticed a glint from something metal on the hill. Most men would have missed it, but Ezra Justice saw it.

Ezra dove from his horse just as a spate of bullets flew over his head. Hitting the ground, he scrambled behind some large rocks and pulled the LaMat from his holster. More bullets whizzed past Ezra's position. The way the bullets were flying, Ezra guessed that there were three shooters on the knoll. Ezra quickly assessed his position and decided where he could get the best advantage even though he was outnumbered.

He slipped from behind one rock to another; with each new location he was sneaking his way closer to the knoll.

One of the Klansmen told another, "Work your way around to the side of him." The man left the knoll, trying to make it to a large rock. As he did, Ezra saw him, fired, and took him down mid-stride with one shot.

The two remaining Klansmen stopped in their tracks, momentarily shocked at seeing their friend go down. Meanwhile, Ezra took off toward another rock, darting behind it just as another round of bullets flew overhead. He ducked down lower behind the rock. When he thought the gunmen might be vulnerable, Ezra rose up slightly and squeezed off several rounds in rapid succession. Every time one of the Klansmen raised his head to fire, Ezra fired first, barely missing their heads. Slowly, he worked his way around to the side of the knoll.

"Do you see him?" one of the gunmen called.

"I'm not sticking my head up there! This was your stupid idea. I'm getting out of here!" The man turned and ran for his horse. The other Klansman realized he didn't want to fight this battle by himself, so he started to run for his horse, as well. But Ezra rose up from the knoll. The man spotted Ezra and started to shoot, but he was too late. Ezra leveled him with a bullet to the chest.

The other man, already fleeing on his horse, fired at Ezra but missed. Ezra spun and fired, catching the man in the shoulder. Wounded, but still alive, the man galloped off as fast as his horse would take him.

Ezra brushed himself off and walked back to find his horse. He reached for his canteen, unhooked it from his saddlebags, and took a long drink. "That was a close one," he said aloud to himself. "Thanks, Lord, for your help." Ezra mounted up again and continued his trip to Lewisburg as though nothing had happened.

The wounded Klansman made it back to town and told Sheriff Cutler about the muffed attempt to kill Ezra Justice. Cutler was furious. The sheriff stormed out of the office and gathered Donlon and four other members of the KKK. "Come on; get your sheets. We're going out there and take care of his darkie friend before Justice returns."

"Yeah," Donlon said, "I've got a score to settle with that fellow. I want to be the one who strings him up. And I'm going to do it slowly!"

AT THE PLANTATION the workers were cleaning debris from the church and trying to salvage whatever they could from the burned-out buildings. As Harry Whitecloud rode onto the plantation, it wasn't hard to spot big Nathaniel York working with the other men.

Harry nudged his horse right up behind Big Nate. "It's good to see you doing some labor for a change," Harry quipped to Nate.

"Harry Whitecloud, you are a sight for sore eyes!" Nate yelled, pulling Harry off the horse with a giant bear hug.

"Good to see you, too, Nate. I'm not even going to ask how you've been doing, but what in the world happened here? I can see you've been having some trouble. Do you want to tell me about it?" Harry asked as he gazed in amazement at the ravaged plantation.

"Come on in the cabin," Nate replied, wiping the sweat from his brow. "I'll get you some water and fill you in on what's been goin' on around here."

EZRA JUSTICE ARRIVED IN LEWISBURG late that same afternoon. He went straight to the telegraph office and sent a message to General Sherman, informing the nation's top military commander how the Ku Klux Klan had been terrorizing innocent people in and around the Pulaski area. Ezra requested that General Sherman authorize the Justice Riders as U.S. marshals.

"I need an immediate response," Ezra wrote at the bottom of the telegram.

He sat down outside the telegram office to await General Sherman's response to his request. As he waited, Ezra reflected on his years growing up on the plantation. It had been a happy place during Ezra's youth, and he and Nate had enjoyed a unique friendship, even though, technically speaking,

Nate and his family members were slaves. But Ezra's family never treated any of their workers as property, so they were not bothered by Ezra's almost brotherly friendship with Nate.

Ezra smiled as he recalled their boyhood. Without Nate he would probably be a lost soul right now. One of the best things Nate had ever done for Ezra was to tell him the truth about Jesus—that he wasn't just a man, but he was God's Son. Nate had helped Ezra realize that the only way he could ever fill the hole in his heart was to have a relationship with God. No wonder Ezra felt indebted to Nate and his family. No wonder Ezra was committed to making sure that Nate and his remaining family members could live in freedom.

"EXCUSE ME, SIR," the telegraph operator's voice brought Ezra back to the crisis at hand. "I believe you have been waiting for this. Here's your telegram."

"Thank you," Ezra said, nodding to the operator. Ezra opened the folded paper and read General Sherman's response: "This telegram officially authorizes the men known as the Justice Riders as U.S. Marshals. Signed, General William Tecumseh Sherman, Commandant, U.S. Army."

Ezra tucked the telegram inside his jacket pocket. It was time to pay a visit to the judge.

SHERIFF DAX CUTLER, John Donlon, and three others dressed in Klan attire with their hoods over their heads rode onto the Justice plantation. They moved quickly right up to Nate's cabin, and as they started to get off their horses, Nate and Harry Whitecloud walked out of the cabin to confront them.

"Who are you, Injun?" Cutler asked.

Whitecloud responded, "A better question is: who are you, such a coward that you can't show your face?"

In a fit of rage, Cutler tore off his own hood. "There! Take a good look, Injun, because it is the last thing you will ever see."

Donlon did the same. "And you take a good look, too, darkie!" he screamed at Nate. "I really wanted to hang you, darkie, but a bullet will have to do!"

Cutler and Donlon went for their guns. They had barely cleared leather before Nate and Whitecloud fired their weapons, putting bullets into Cutler and Donlon's chests. The other three Klansmen reared back in their saddles, shocked to see their comrades tumbling from their horses.

With the barrels of their guns still smoking and pointing at the remaining Klansmen, Nate and Harry stood ready to fan their revolvers. They waited a moment to see whether the Klansmen were going to go for their guns or do the smart thing and surrender.

The Klansmen made the wrong choice. They went for their guns.

In an instant Nate York and Harry Whitecloud fanned the hammers of their already cocked guns, dropping the three white-sheeted figures as the Klansmen's bullets sprayed wildly into the air.

Harry looked down at the five sheet-covered bodies on the ground. "Well, Nate," Harry said, "that's a good start."

LATE THAT NIGHT Ezra returned to the plantation, happy to see the first of four Justice Riders had arrived.

"I'm glad you could make it, Harry," Ezra said.

"Well, I'm glad I made it when I did. Otherwise I might have missed the fun," Harry said, pointing to the five bodies laid out on the ground.

"What happened?"

"I think the sheriff and his men came out to string me up while you were gone," Nate said. "Luckily, Harry was here to lend his support."

"Nate has filled me in a bit about what has been going on around here," Harry said.

"Good, then you realize that we need the other Justice Riders," said Ezra.

"They'll be here, Captain. You can count on it," Whitecloud promised.

THE FOLLOWING MORNING Ezra, Nate, and Whitecloud took the five bodies of the dead Klansmen to the undertaker in Pulaski. They then went to Judge Black's office, walking right in without being announced. Black was in a meeting with Harris, Shaw, and Evans.

"I believe you men are the leaders of the Ku Klux Klan in this area," Ezra said, "and you should know that my men and I have been authorized by General William T. Sherman as U.S. marshals. We're going to arrest anyone we find with a white sheet and hood. We're going to make this county safe for everyone—black or white." As the Justice Riders turned to leave, Ezra stopped in front of Judge Black and said, "By the way, you need a new sheriff. The old one is at the undertaker's." Ezra and his men walked out of the office while Judge Black and his men stared behind them, their mouths hanging open in surprise.

At first Judge Black tried to talk, but his mouth refused to form actual words. When he finally overcame his initial shock, he jumped up from his chair and flew into a rage, pacing back and forth across the room, cursing and yelling. He finally stopped and turned to the men in front of him. "Alert every member of the Klan and tell them to meet at 2:00 Thursday morning at the Greenwood Grove. That gives you two days to contact all the members. We're going to destroy everything that's left of the Justice plantation and hang everyone on it that we haven't already shot! And that includes those U.S. marshals."

Andrew Shaw looked up from where he was seated. Shaw couldn't believe his own ears. "Judge, surely you don't mean those words literally," the newspaper man said. "You can't do that! You can't kill U.S. marshals. And you can't hang all those people out there on the plantation."

"Yes, I can, Andrew. And I fully intend to. And I want you to know that anyone who doesn't show up at the gathering will be considered in league with the enemy and will be dealt with. This is not a request. It is an order! Do you get my meaning, Andrew?"

"Yeah, I get your meaning," Andrew said quietly.

"Now get out of here, and make sure that everyone is notified," Judge Black said. "And tell them to bring their sheets, masks, and hoods." The men exited the room without a word.

EZRA, NATE, AND WHITECLOUD sat around an old table, strategizing how to counter Judge Black's next move, when the Hawkins twins rode up.

"Well, it seems quiet enough out here living in the country," Carlos said. "Except everything's burned down."

"Isn't it amazing how observant my brother is," Roberto said, shaking his head.

"Well, observe yourselves off your horses and get over here," Nate responded.

After some hugs of greeting, Ezra quickly brought the Hawkins twins up to speed regarding the recent events in Pulaski and on the plantation. Ezra told them that Judge Black, the man he was sure was the leader of the Klan, would pull out all the stops now. "He realizes the survival of the Klan depends on putting us down," Ezra said somberly. "There will be no peaceful getting along. It's either us or them."

WORD WENT OUT QUICKLY to Ku Klux Klan members all over the surrounding area. Some of them expressed their hesitancy to be involved in Black's plan when they were contacted, but they were quickly convinced that they didn't have a choice. "Black and his men will hunt you down and kill you if you fail the Klan now," the messengers threatened.

THE JUSTICE RIDERS were cleaning their weapons when a lone rider approached the plantation.

"Who's that?" Carlos Hawkins asked, cocking his weapon. "Is he one of your boys?"

"He's not one of ours," Nate said. "You better shout out who you are, Mister, before we shoot you out of the saddle!" Nate called loudly.

"Don't shoot, don't shoot," a trembling voice said. "It's Andrew Shaw, from the newspaper."

"Get down, Mr. Shaw," Ezra said.

Shaw dismounted and limped toward Justice. The possessor of a permanent limp thanks to the earlier fall from his horse, Andrew Shaw made his way toward the place where the Justice Riders were sitting.

"What can we do for you, Mr. Shaw?" Ezra Justice asked, spinning the chambers on his revolver as he spoke.

"I just want to let you know that I am no longer a member of the Ku Klux Klan," Shaw spoke nervously. "And I wanted to tell you that Judge Black is completely out of control. He is gathering all the Klan members in this area at the Greenwood Grove, and they are coming here to your plantation to kill everyone."

"When are they gathering?" Ezra asked.

"At two tomorrow morning."

"Wow, we got here just in time," Carlos said to Roberto.

Andrew Shaw continued, "I never thought it would come to this. Judge Black has gone insane with his hatred of you darkies . . . Negroes," he said, looking at Nate. "I don't want anything else to do with it.

"They will probably kill me when they find out that I warned you, but now you have time to get everyone off the plantation and get away before they get here."

"Mr. Shaw, I can promise you that the Klan will not kill you," Ezra said.

"I hope you are right, Mr. Justice." Andrew Shaw mounted his horse and rode out into the darkness.

Justice shook his head as he watched Shaw go. "The sad part of all this, men, is that many of the Klan members are people a lot like Shaw. They may not be in favor of liberating the Negroes, but they are tolerant of it. Unfortunately, they are being led by evil people."

At 1:00 in the morning, Ezra and the others were preparing to leave for Greenwood Grove outside Pulaski when Reginald Bonesteel rode onto the Justice plantation. Carlos and Roberto said almost in unison, "Bonesteel, you are always late!"

"Late? Late for what?"

"We'll tell you on the way, Reginald," Ezra said. "Welcome back. Thanks for coming."

A LARGE CROWD OF Klan members assembled at Greenwood Grove, wearing their Klan sheets and holding their hoods in their hands. Many of the men carried flaming torches as well, lighting the grove almost as brightly as daylight, even though it was the middle of the night.

Judge Black stepped up onto a makeshift speaker's platform to address the more than sixty men who had gathered.

"For far too long we have been tolerating the rebellious behavior of these slaves who have been sent into this world to do our bidding. We have fed them, clothed them, and housed them. But do they appreciate our benevolence?"

"No!" the crowd of Klansmen roared, their attention riveted on Judge Black.

"No, they do not!" Black bellowed. "And now, with the help of some white traitors, they are plotting an uprising like none of us have ever imagined possible in our fair city of Pulaski, an uprising in which the darkies actually want to own property and would love for us to work for them! We must stop this and stop it now!"

"That's right!" a rough-sounding voice called out in the night. "Stop them now. Now or never!"

Black raised his arms, and the crowd of white-sheet-covered men grew silent. He continued, "And sad to say, one of our own citizens, a man who was raised right here in these parts, Mr. Ezra Justice, has been the main facilitator of this uprising of the darkies. He and his so-called marshals are itching for a confrontation, and tonight they are going to get it."

Judge Black's voice grew loud and shrill in pitch. "We are going out to the Justice plantation tonight. We will hang as many darkies as we can and shoot the rest. And as for Justice and his men, let me put it this way: when we are done tonight, I don't want to see a darkie or a darkie lover anywhere on that plantation. Kill them all! Women and children, too."

Judge Black was screaming now. "Wake up, white people, wake up! We must put the darkies in their place . . . which is in the ground . . . because the only good darkie is a dead darkie!"

The Klan started chanting, "White is might; white is right! White is might; white is right!"

"Now is the time!" Judge Black roared. "Now put on your hoods; take up your torches; it is time!"

Just as Judge Stanton Black had worked the crowd into a frenzy, suddenly, from out of the shadows, a lone Klansman, covered in a white sheet and wearing a white hood over his head, walked casually onto the platform, right over to where the judge was standing.

Surprised at the interruption, Black stared at the white-sheeted figure and said, "What can I do for you?"

"It's not what you can do for me, Judge," the figure answered. "It's what I'm gonna do to you." The man ripped off the sheet and hood, revealing a LaMat aimed right at Judge Black's heart. Ezra Justice waved the LaMat at Black as he looked down at the sixty plus men staring up at him in shock. "You are under arrest by the authority of the U.S. marshals," Justice said.

Black peered at Justice like he could not believe his eyes and ears. "I have sixty men here, Justice," Black spat out, "who are going to hang you and everyone on that plantation."

"There's going to be a hanging, alright, Judge," Ezra said, "but it is going to be the people responsible for the hanging of four innocent men."

"You talk big for one man, even if you are a U.S. marshal," Black said derisively.

"He can talk big, Judge, because he has five more U.S. marshals to back him up," Reginald Bonesteel stepped up to say. Nate, Whitecloud, Bonesteel, and the Hawkins twins came in with their guns drawn, stepping out from behind the Klansmen from five other angles and five different directions. "I'm sure you have heard of the Justice Riders," Bonesteel continued. "Well, you are looking down the barrels of six of them right now."

"We've killed more than all of you without working up a sweat," said Carlos Hawkins.

Ezra continued, "Now take off your hoods or draw your guns. Either way is fine with us."

Slowly, one man at a time, the Klansmen began removing their hoods. Black turned and glared at Ezra. "You'll never get a conviction."

Ezra slammed his fist into Black's jaw, dropping him like a rock. "If I want your opinion, Judge, I'll beat it out of you."

The Justice Riders collected the Klansmens' weapons and marched the hoodless Klansmen back to town. The sun was just coming up as the men wearing white sheets dragged themselves into downtown Pulaski.

"Nate, you and Bonesteel put the judge, Harris, and Evans in the jailhouse," Ezra commanded.

The families of the Klansmen had gathered in town, nervously waiting for their men to return. Word had gotten out already that something big was happening, but nobody expected to see the parade of some of Pulaski's leading citizens—all wearing Ku Klux Klan outfits—being marched up the main street of town at gunpoint by six U.S. marshals. For the first time ever, the community learned the truth about who had been involved in the Klan, and the Klansmen were exposed as the cowardly bigots they truly were.

A large number of Negroes from in and around Pulaski had also dared to assemble in the presence of the Klan. Now, as the Negroes watched the humiliated Klansmen march through the streets, they realized that the Klansmen were not ghosts or gods; they were mere men—cowardly men, at that—men who drew their power from fear and intimidation rather than love and service. Seeing the Klansmen for what they really were sparked new fires of freedom within the hearts of many of the Negroes watching the proceedings that morning.

Gathering the Klansmen in front of the courthouse, Ezra Justice stepped up onto the courthouse steps to speak to the crowd.

"You may have done things differently in the past. I know many of you have a deep hatred of the Negroes, and you believe that they should still be slaves. But the war is over, and the slaves are freed. And that is the law of the land.

"You are welcome to your own opinions; this is a free country. It doesn't matter to me how you think, but it does matter to me what you do. If you do anything to the Negroes, or to anyone else for that matter, that goes against the laws of our nation, you will be prosecuted to the fullest extent of the law."

Justice looked at the crowd of men in white sheets huddled in front of him. "I'm going to let you go this time, except for the ringleaders of this Klan. They will be prosecuted. I've summoned a federal judge to Pulaski, and Judge Stanton Black, Archibald Harris, Doctor Howard Evans, and their accomplices will be tried for the murder of four innocent men."

Ezra paused and looked directly at the men in the white sheets. "The rest of you have a second chance. You can change your ways, or you can face the threat of justice. I can't change your hearts—only God can do that—but I can tell you this: the violence against the Negroes ends now." Ezra paused and looked around at the large crowd. "Do you understand me? It ends *now!*"

The crowd of onlookers burst into cheers, a number of men throwing their hats in the air. Many of the women hugged each other or their children, and several people broke down in tears of relief.

"Mama, why are you crying?" one little girl asked her mother.

"Because our town is truly free for the first time in a long, long time," the mother said.

Justice waved his hand above his head, and the noise subsided. "I have one more thing to say. The Justice Riders are now U.S. marshals. We have shown these offenders grace when they deserved to be punished. But don't ever interpret grace as license to do evil. If we have to come back and deal with this kind of prejudice and injustice again, we will not be as lenient next time. Now go to your homes and live in peace."

Two days later the Hawkins twins, Reginald Bonesteel, and Harry Whitecloud were back at the plantation, sitting around the table, trying to decide what to do next. "I guess that panning for gold isn't as easy as everyone says it is, huh Reginald?" Roberto asked.

"Oh, I wouldn't say that," Bonesteel replied. "Of course, I was just getting the hang of it when I received Elizabeth's telegram. I had already discovered two sizable chunks of gold. Had I remained there, given enough time, I have no doubt that I would have found my fortune."

"That's not what you told me, Reginald," Carlos interrupted. "You said you were broke, cold, and nearly starving to death out there in California."

"Ah-hem, thank you very much, Carlos," Bonesteel eyed him, "for that most encouraging report." Reginald Bonesteel laughed lightly. "But to tell you the truth, I'm glad to be back with you boys again. Panning for gold is too boring for me. How about you, Harry? How did you fare in medical school?"

Harry Whitecloud flicked his long hair over his shoulder. "Well, the classes were interesting, but I found as much prejudice there as Ezra and Nate found here in Pulaski. It simply takes different forms."

"Will you be going back soon?" Bonesteel asked.

"I guess that all depends on what Ezra has in mind," Harry said. "Now that we're U.S. marshals, I've been having some second thoughts about returning to Princeton right now. I still want to help my people, the Sioux; but to tell you the truth, it was mighty nice to be back working with the Justice Riders again. What about you two?" Harry nodded toward Carlos and Roberto.

"Well, as luck would have it," Roberto replied, "ours ran out."

"Yeah, and our money did, too," Carlos added.

Just then Ezra and Nate came riding in from town. They dismounted and handed the reins of their horses to one of the workers, who watered the animals and took them to the carriage house.

Ezra and Nate walked up to the four other Justice Riders. "This looks like a serious discussion, men. What's going on?" Ezra asked.

"Well, Captain, we were just wondering: What are we going to do now?" Bonesteel asked.

"Well, the first thing Nate and I are going to do . . ." Ezra stopped and called all the workers over to the carriage house. "Nate has an announcement to make," Ezra said.

"Oh, Ezra, why me?" Nate asked, embarrassed. "It was your idea."

"Yeah, but you agreed."

"Alright, alright," Nate gave in. "Sophie, Mr. Justice and I have deeded the plantation over to you and all the other people who have made this plantation what it once was. And now you can make it again what it should be. The Justice plantation now belongs to you all!"

The crowd of workers was stunned at first, and then when they realized the ramifications of what Ezra and Nate had done, everyone started cheering, whooping it up, and laughing with joy. The workers and their family members all started hugging Ezra, Nate, and one another—amazed and grateful that the former slaves were all now landowners.

Sophie stood up and said, "Nate, and Mr. Justice, on behalf of all of us who have lived and worked here on the Justice plantation, I want to thank you from the bottom of our hearts. Not just for the land, Mr. Justice—as generous as your gift is—but for respecting us as people. May God always bless you."

The crowd slowly dissipated as the people excitedly began making plans for what needed to be done on the plantation.

"That still doesn't answer my question," Reginald Bonesteel spoke up. "What are we going to do now?"

Nate said, "Well, since we are U.S. marshals, let's go get our badges from General Sherman."

"And where will we go after that?" Carlos asked.

"Wherever anybody has need of us," said Ezra Justice.

Six U.S. marshals—also known as the Justice Riders—mounted up and rode off into the sunset, confident that new and exciting adventures awaited them on every trail ahead.

Turn the page for an exciting preview of

THE JUSTICE RIDERS

the first book in
THE JUSTICE RIDERS SERIES

Available now
ISBN: 978-0-8054-4430-8
www.BHPublishingGroup.com

From
THE JUSTICE RIDERS

Captain Ezra Justice dove for cover just as the vanguard of General Joe Johnston's Confederate Army rounded the bend, coming out of the small North Carolina town of Bentonville, headed northward toward Richmond. Lying on the ground, shrouded by a clump of bushes, Justice stiffened as he heard a sound behind him; his finger tightened on the trigger of his LaMat nine-shot revolver. From behind the bushes emerged a tall, muscular black man, dressed in a Union soldier's uniform, complete with a blue kepi cap and perfectly tied dark blue bow tie. Crouching low, he made his way toward Ezra. Justice relaxed his grip on the LaMat.

Nathaniel York—"Big Nate," as he'd been known most of his life and still was—flopped down on the grass next to Justice. "Everything's in position, Cap'n," he said. "We're ready when you are."

"OK, fine. Good work, Nate."

"Shades of Washington all over again, huh?" Nate pointed down the hillside toward the long rows of Confederate infantry soldiers now coming into view, with the supply line behind them.

"Let's hope so," Justice said, raising his eyebrows slightly and nodding.

Nate understood the look of concern on Ezra's face. The scene below was reminiscent of General Joe Johnston's forces coming to the aid of P. G. T. Beauregard's Confederate army at Manassas in late July of 1861. Johnston's army thwarted the Union forces advancing southward from Washington, not only beating them back but sending them on the run, forcing them to retreat all the way to the Capitol. Had it not been for a dispute between Johnston and Confederate President Jefferson Davis, Johnston might have marched right into Washington and the war might have turned in an entirely different direction.

Davis's badly timed intervention, combined with problems in the supply lines—caused mainly by covert attacks and diversions spawned by Ezra Justice and his band of marauders—stymied the Confederates' offensive action toward Washington and gave the Federal army a much-needed opportunity to regroup and reposition its forces.

Now, more than three years later, with the South reeling from a series of devastating military blows, General Johnston's battle-weary but undaunted troops were threatening to change the course of the war again. And Johnston believed he would succeed in his assignment at all costs.

Equally determined to stop Johnston's army from reinforcing General Robert E. Lee's was a quiet but courageous captain in the Union Army, Ezra Justice. General William T. Sherman had personally assigned Justice and his men—all six of them—to stand in Johnston's way, to slow down an entire army, to do everything possible—anything possible—to interrupt Johnston's northern progress.

MORE THAN ANY MAN ALIVE, Nathaniel York knew how to interpret the often understated expressions of his enigmatic leader, Ezra Justice. Nate raised a finger to his thin, neatly trimmed mustache as though contemplating some great philosophical truth. "Think we can pull this off, Ezra?"

Justice didn't flinch at the sergeant's familiarity. Most of the other men rarely referred to their leader by his first name, but Nathaniel York was not just a fellow soldier. He and Ezra were best friends, practically family. They'd grown up together on a large, prosperous Tennessee tobacco farm owned by Ezra's parents. Nathaniel York, however, was a former slave, legally emancipated by Abraham Lincoln, but emancipated a long time before that by his friend Ezra Justice. Even as a boy, Ezra had believed that all men were created equal and had defied his family's ironclad rules for relating to "darkies." Against his parents' objections, he had formed a strong bond of friendship with Nate. Now, with both men fighting for the North, that friendship remained intact.

Moreover, Nathaniel York hailed from good roots. His grandfather—also a slave—had gained great respect and admiration as a member of the Lewis and Clark expedition in 1803. For his part, Nathaniel York never thought of himself as enslaved to anybody, despite the fact that his family worked long hours in the tobacco fields and lived in a shack at the back of the Justice property. Bright, articulate, and deeply spiritual, Nathaniel had committed his life to God as a boy and had adopted Jesus' statement, "The truth will set you free" as his motto. When Ezra asked Big Nate to join him in setting other men free, Nate never hesitated. He'd fought throughout the war, a black man and a white man side by side, with his friend Ezra Justice.

Ezra peered down at the seemingly endless line of soldiers streaming out of the town. Getting to the supply line would not be easy, he knew. Getting out with their lives would be tougher still. He spoke to himself as much as to Nate. "We have to stop them, Nate. We have to stop them here."

"Yes, sir. Word from the North is that General Grant has Lee ready to do something desperate."

"It's about time," Justice replied. "That siege at Petersburg has been going on for far too long. For the past ten months, our men have been living in trenches all the way from Petersburg to Richmond. Grant's been puttin' the squeeze on them, and Lee's boys are getting nervous. General Joe Johnston's army in North Carolina is the South's last hope. If we can keep Johnston's troops from reinforcing Lee's, we might be able to bring this war to a close. If we can't . . ." Ezra's voice trailed off.

"If we can't?" Nate pressed.

"If Johnston gets his troops to General Lee, they will be a formidable force against General Grant's army. They may be able to mount an attack that will split Grant's troops and break the siege. If they do that, a lot more men are going to die on both sides."

Nate nodded and proceeded to brief Ezra on the readiness report. "Sergeant Bonesteel has his .44-caliber rifle scope focused on the first ammunition wagon. Sergeant Whitecloud has his own brand of Injun fireworks ready on the other side of town. He can't wait to get into the fight. I practically had to hold him down when he saw those Confederate cavalry boys.

"And the Hawkins twins are itching to try out their new invention they dreamed up for our enjoyment. Some wacky thing they call a 'satchel charge.'" Justice smiled at Nate's sarcasm regarding Roberto and Carlos Hawkins, two of the most ingenious young explosives experts he'd ever known. Nate would have been content to rely on good old-fashioned dynamite charges, but not the twins. The Hawkins brothers were constantly coming up with seemingly ridiculous new methods to destroy something, and Ezra had learned long ago not to be so cynical. The twins' crazy inventions usually worked. *Usually*.

Nate interrupted Ezra's ruminations. "And O'Banyon wants to go down and try to talk them into surrendering."

Ezra's mouth hinted at a smile as he thought of Shaun O'Banyon, the lovable, impetuous Irishman who in the past had preferred a bottle of good whiskey over fighting any day. Shaun O'Banyon believed that he could talk his way out of most any situation, and he often did. But this would not be a day for talk.

"Pass the word, Nathaniel. When the church bell strikes three, let 'er rip. There's no way the seven of us can stand a chance against their entire army. Our goal is to slow them down by taking out their supplies. Try not to get involved in combat with their troops any more than necessary. Otherwise we will lose our element of surprise. We have to hit them hard and fast. Get in quickly and get out. If we take more than a few minutes, we're all dead men."

Nate rose to his knees. "Got it, Cap'n." He halfway stood up, brushed himself off, and repeated the command. "Start the attack right after the bell strikes three. I'll meet you back at the camp. God be with ya, Ezra."

Ezra nodded but didn't look around as Nate slipped away. "Here's hoping."

GENERAL JOE JOHNSTON'S TROOPS never knew what hit them. One moment they were trudging through town, complaining about their aching feet and how much farther they had to go before meeting up with General Lee; the next moment, just after three o'clock, when the church bell tolled for the third time, the earth erupted. Preset dynamite charges blew dozens of soldiers closest to the supply train sky high. Many of the multiple sticks of dynamite tied together and buried just below the ground exploded almost simultaneously due to some long fuses rigged before sun-up and now ignited by Harry Whitecloud. Huge craters ripped open in front of the supply train, bringing it to a halt.

From his concealed location in the hills, Reginald Bonesteel squeezed the trigger on his Henry .44-caliber repeating rifle. The butt of the high-powered rifle kicked hard against Bonesteel's shoulder, but the British-born marksman kept on firing. A moment later, an enormous explosion blew the first ammunitions wagon into a ball of flame. A second concussion followed, creating several more deafening blasts. By the third and fourth rounds, bits of fiery wood were flying through the air, landing on the ammo wagons following behind, igniting the canvas atop the arms wagons and turning that section of the road into an inferno as well. Satisfied with his work, Bonesteel mounted his horse and kneed it toward the fire. With a double set of holsters strapped on the front of his saddle and another double set of guns behind the saddle, Bonesteel swept through a line of Confederate officers at full gallop, firing incessantly in every direction as he crossed the road. Men in gray uniforms who had been maneuvering the troops, in their efforts to fend off the attack, dropped in Bonesteel's path. A piece of shell winged the brazen Brit in his shoulder, but it didn't slow him down a bit. His steed's powerful legs stretched out as though in a race for dear life, and Bonesteel disappeared into the forest on the other side of the field.

The sky around the supply train turned a gritty brown laced with orange. The acrid smell of burnt gunpowder permeated the air. The flames and smoke created so much chaos and confusion in the Confederate ranks that nobody noticed the lone rider racing toward the water wagons. When a soldier finally caught a glimpse of the rider wearing a blue jacket and a wide-brimmed hat, it was too late. The man on the horse blew the soldier into eternity. He flipped a lever on his specially designed LaMat, and the single shot pistol became a blazing rapid-firing repeater. Good thing, too. Ezra Justice needed all the firepower he could get. Three or four Confederate soldiers converged on him, but Ezra eluded them. Justice felled several more gray-coats as he dodged the musket balls whizzing by his ears. He took comfort in one of his own favorite sayings that he used often with his men: "Don't worry about the lead you hear. If you hear the bullet, it's already gone by you. It's the one you don't hear that you have to worry about."

Ezra knew that merely upsetting the wagon carrying the large barrels laden with water wouldn't be good enough. He wanted to destroy General Johnston's water supply. An army can survive a long time without food but only a few days without water. Even if the troops kept moving northward, they'd have to stop for water before long, giving General Grant more precious time to drive toward Richmond.

At full gallop Ezra reached the water wagons and started firing, not at the soldiers nearby but at the barrels containing the water. One by one, streams of water poured out of the barrels as, too late, the Rebels realized the true targets of Ezra Justice's bullets. With his gun barrel hot, Justice danced his horse through the maze of dead bodies, mangled wagons, and other equipment. Getting to the supply line was one thing; getting clear of it would be quite another.

Ezra veered hard to the left, attempting to avoid several Rebs running back toward the supply train. His horse obediently leaped over a pile of rubble as Ezra pulled up hard on the reins. Just as he went airborne, he saw the soldier in the dirty gray coat, kneeling on the ground straight ahead of him, aiming his musket right at Justice. Ezra tried to duck, but it was too late. He heard the sound of a rifle blast.

The kneeling soldier crumpled to the dirt as the hoofs of Ezra's horse touched the ground. Ezra looked behind him and saw Nathaniel York coming alongside, smoke still curling from the barrel of his carbine. "Thanks, Nate. That was a close one."

"Glad to be of service!" Nate yelled as he galloped by toward the chow wagons without breaking stride. Nate pulled a sawed-off 12-gauge shotgun out of his saddle holster and blasted his way toward the food supply. Confederate soldiers scattered or dropped to the ground as the feared shotgun sprayed pellets in a wide swath. The shotgun blast gave Nate just the opening he needed to get close to the mess wagons. He lit a torch on the way by and tossed it onto the top of one of the covered wagons carrying the food supplies.

Whooosh! The wagon burst into flames.

Shaun O'Banyon had worked his way to the rear of the supply line where the extra horses were in tow. His job, although relatively easy in the midst of the chaos, was one of the most dangerous. He wanted to set the horses free, to stampede them hopefully in the opposite direction of Richmond, so even if the Confederates were able to round them up again, the time it took to track down and capture the horses would disrupt the army's forward progress.

While the confusion raged up ahead at the front of the supply train, O'Banyon raised his head up out of the ditch in which he had been waiting impatiently. He spotted the horses about to come by, roped to several feed wagons. Taking careful aim from his position, O'Banyon picked off three men struggling to keep the horses calm that were pulling the feed wagons. He then quickly mounted his wild-eyed Appaloosa horse, which had been hidden behind a thicket. Before anyone saw him coming, O'Banyon came out of nowhere and boldly made for the horses.

Pulling up in front of the feed wagon, O'Banyon couldn't resist commiserating with the animals. "Such a pity to be agitating these fine animals," he said, as he slashed the reins previously securing two large beauties to the wagon. "Get on, now! Go south." O'Banyon slapped the rear flanks of the biggest horse. "Go now! You've seen enough of this kind of fightin'. You've served these Johnny Rebs for too long. Today, I'll be giving you your own emancipation proclamation. Go, Big Fella! Go, Sweet Lady. Go visit General Sherman or just go find a wee bit of green." One by one, O'Banyon went down the row of horses, slashing the reins, offering a few words of encouragement or a friendly pat to each animal before slapping it on its way southward. When the last horse had been freed, O'Banyon spurred his own animal, which reared slightly and took off through the haze of spherical lead balls flying all around him.

Meanwhile, Ezra Justice headed toward the twelve-pound round-shot howitzers, each with its own large ammo box being pulled on the same wagon wheels as the huge gun barrel. Ezra ducked just as a hot piece of shrapnel flew by his head. He heard a sickening thud as the metal seared into a young Confederate lieutenant, hitting him chest high, shredding his upper shoulder and mangling his left arm. Ezra Justice flinched as he saw the boy fall on his face. Ezra hated this war, with its senseless maiming and killing; but there was nothing he could do but hope that by doing his job well, he could help bring it to an end soon.

Ezra glanced in the direction of the front lines. Time was running out.

Although only a minute or two had passed since the first shots had been fired, by now, Rebel infantrymen and, beyond them, the Cavalrymen had realized the true nature of the attack and were doubling back to help their fallen comrades. The Confederate soldiers had been caught with their guard down, but those who had survived the initial blasts were scrambling to defend the supply train with any weapon available.

Pulling two sticks of dynamite from his saddlebags as he rode, Justice was about to light the fuse and toss it toward the howitzers when a soldier on the ground grabbed a shovel, hauled off and swung the blade at Ezra's midsection, walloping Justice right in the stomach, knocking him off his horse and sending him tumbling to the ground face first. For a moment Ezra's world went dark, then he felt the dirt and blood in his mouth. Holding his side, Ezra thought sure that a rib was broken. *No time to worry about it now.* He spit out some blood and staggered to his feet, just in time to elude the soldier diving toward him, bowie knife in hand. Undaunted, the soldier came at Ezra again.

Ignoring the pain in his side, Ezra pivoted on his left foot. Instantly, he whirled around a full 180 degrees and launched his right leg at the man's face, connecting his right foot squarely with the soldier's jaw, flipping him backward in the air and landing him on his side with a grunt, right next to a dead Confederate soldier. Ezra's attacker raised up, leaning momentarily on his left hand, sliding his right hand over the dead soldier. Still a bit groggy himself, Ezra almost didn't see the Rebel snatch the dead man's revolver off the ground, fumbling to aim it at Justice. In a flash, Justice's strong right arm chopped down, the straightened side of his rigid, bare hand connecting firmly on the side of his attacker's neck. Ezra stood over him, waiting to see if he was going to retaliate. The soldier didn't get up; he was out cold.

That's when Ezra saw Mordecai Slate for the first time.

Off to Ezra's left a Cavalry officer sat on a black horse, amidst the burning rubble, smoke, and dust of battle, the blackened remains of a supply wagon behind him. Dressed in full, clean Confederate regalia, while his soldiers wore filthy, tattered trousers and shoes with gaping holes in them, the officer was ruggedly handsome yet possessed a nearly palpable sense of malice at the same time—the type of man that men feared and women could not resist. Although he had never met him, Ezra recognized the officer immediately. He'd heard about Mordecai Slate, a leader who preferred to fight out front with his men, rather than remaining in safety behind the artillery lines. Known as a ferocious and merciless soldier, Slate was the commander of a regiment detached from the rest of the Confederate army, a regiment that nobody on either side of the Mason-Dixon line wanted to claim—"the Death Raiders" regiment, as they were known.

At one time, the band of thugs under Slate's command may have been honorable soldiers of the South. At one time . . . maybe . . . but not anymore. Mordecai Slate had slowly but surely transformed his regiment from noble men fighting for a cause they believed in to murderers who enjoyed killing for no reason or any reason. They took no prisoners, preferring to shoot anyone they captured rather than bother with having to feed, house, and/or transport the enemy.

Slate sat high on his horse, his revolver aimed at Ezra's chest. "Justice!" he called. "How about some of Mordecai Slate's brand of justice?"

Ezra looked up and saw Mordecai Slate pull the trigger and felt the bullet slam into his chest. The impact of the bullet sent Justice reeling backward onto the ground. His body didn't move; his face was expressionless.

Mordecai Slate let out a hideous laugh, spinning his horse and galloping back to the fracas.

CHARGING AT FULL SPEED, Roberto and Carlos Hawkins streaked down the supply train, one on each side of the row of howitzers. Attached to the boys' saddles were two large satchels. Roberto's horse jumped, and Roberto's arm raised high, revealing a long knife in his hand. His arm slashed downward, toward the side of the saddle, and the bag dropped to the ground, landing just under the howitzer's ammo box.

No sooner had Roberto's horse landed in stride, than the first satchel exploded beneath the howitzer. The force of the explosion sent cannonballs flying in all directions, as well as igniting fires all along the supply line. A moment later Carlos delivered his first satchel charge, his horse leaping a cannon on a dead run. Carlos whacked the satchel away from his saddle directly above the cannon. He knew he had only a second or two before the charge went off. The back legs of his horse barely touched the ground when the bag exploded—fortunately in the opposite direction from the one in which Carlos was jumping. The Hawkins boys crisscrossed the artillery lines, delivering two more satchel charges and leaving a trail of death and destruction behind them as the Confederate ammunition supplies went up in smoke.

Harry Whitecloud was racing by, shooting fire arrows into the canvas-covered ammunition wagons when he spotted Ezra Justice lying deathly still on the ground. Harry sprang off his horse, and the well-trained animal came to an immediate halt. Harry ran to Ezra, praying that his captain was still alive but expecting to find him dead. He knelt down and rolled Justice over on his back. Ezra's face was caked with dirt and blood. Harry's worst fears were realized when he saw the ragged bullet hole that had pierced Ezra Justice's jacket just above his heart.

Whitecloud had seen death many times, but something about Ezra Justice caused Harry to regard him as invulnerable. *This can't be happening. This man is indestructible,* Harry thought. "I'm not going to leave you here, Captain," Harry said aloud. The strong Indian grasped Justice by the shoulders, preparing to hoist Ezra onto his horse. As he did, he heard a low groan emanating from the captain.

"You're alive!" Harry cried.

Ezra struggled to sit up. "Yeah, barely," he said hoarsely. He reached inside his breast pocket and pulled out a gold pocket watch. Lodged dead center in the watch was a flattened .44-caliber slug.

Whitecloud looked at Ezra in amazement. "Captain, you are shot full of luck."

"It's more than luck, Harry," Ezra said as he slowly stood to his feet. "Now let's get back to the cabin."

Ezra looked around and saw destruction and dead bodies everywhere. The stench of war, burning flesh, and acrid smoke burned his eyes. The one man Ezra did not see was Mordecai Slate. Somehow, in the rain of lead and cannon and the haze of dust and smoke, Mordecai Slate had disappeared. Ezra's stomach churned. He had a feeling he'd meet Mordecai Slate again.

Ezra whistled for his horse, grabbed onto the saddle horn, and pulled himself onto his mount. He winced at the pain in his chest as he straightened up in the saddle.

Harry leaped onto his horse and looked back over his shoulder at Justice. "A guy could get hurt around here," Harry deadpanned. Without breaking stride, they maneuvered their horses through the smoke and fire, past the remaining supply depot guards, and toward the safety of the forest across the field.

A few moments later Harry and Ezra were out of harm's way. Ezra turned around long enough to look back at the devastation he and his rogue band of soldiers had caused. All along the supply train fire and smoke filled the air and burning debris littered the ground. Harry and Ezra slowed their stallions to a trot, and Ezra reached into his coat pocket and pulled out the gold pocket watch his father had given him as a young man. Ezra flipped open the watch's lid and smiled. Mordecai Slate's bullet had stopped the timepiece at barely seven minutes past three.

ONE BY ONE, Ezra's men picked their way through the woods and made their way back to their previously agreed upon meeting spot. Harry and Ezra were the first to arrive at the camp, an abandoned cabin deep in the North Carolina forest. They were followed shortly by Reginald Bonesteel.

"How'd you make out, Bonesteel?" Ezra asked as he helped the always particular Englishman unload the four holsters from his horse.

"A most enjoyable afternoon, Captain." Bonesteel dismounted and pulled his rifle out of a side pocket on his saddle.

He stroked the .44-caliber's long barrel as though he were caressing a pet. "Henry here was magnificent."

"Come on inside, Mr. Bonesteel. Let's see how bad that wound is. I'd hate to see you get any more blood on your uniform." Ezra smiled as Bonesteel gazed in surprise at the dark blue spot on his coat, where blood was oozing from his shoulder. Ezra correctly guessed that Reginald Bonesteel had nearly forgotten that he had been winged during the fracas.

"Sit down over there." Ezra nodded toward a stool in front of the fireplace. Bonesteel shed his double-breasted coat and shirt, revealing his muscular upper body and hard-as-a-rock chest. As a former member of the Queen of England's personal bodyguard, Bonesteel had been selected to that honored position as much for his striking good looks and powerful physique as for his uncanny skill with a rifle.

Justice poured some water into a cracked bowl and brought it over to Bonesteel. "Sit still. Let's see where that bullet is." He wiped the blood away from Bonesteel's wound, and with a small set of tongs he pulled the lead out of Bonesteel's shoulder. Bonesteel winced but didn't say a word. Fortunately, the musket ball hadn't penetrated too deeply. Justice found an old bedsheet and ripped it into strips of cloth that he used as bandages to stop Bonesteel's bleeding.

"We're both very fortunate today, Reginald."

"Let's hope it stays that way, Captain."

Nate came through the cabin door next. His usually immaculate uniform was soiled and torn, but otherwise the big man was intact. "Those Rebs are going to be stuck here for quite a while, Captain. Even if they do get to Richmond, General Grant will have plenty of time to get ready for them."

Ezra glanced up from where he was still working on Bonesteel's wound. "That's what we wanted to accomplish, Nate. Good work. And thanks for saving my life out there."

"Aw, it was nothin', Cap'n. You'd do the same for me."

Justice looked his friend in the eyes. "That goes without saying, Nate."

THE HAWKINS TWINS WERE LAUGHING in youthful enthusiasm as they turned their horses toward the cabin. "We've never come up with any weapon quite like those satchel charges," Roberto said, shaking his head. "Were they amazing or what?"

"Maybe so," Carlos replied. "But next time, let's allow another second or two before the charge goes off. That last one singed the hair on my neck."

"Ha, you're lucky that's all it did," Roberto fired back. "I hope there's something to eat and drink in this place. I'm starved!"

Inside the cabin Ezra Justice and his soldiers heartily embraced, locking arms in an expression that said more than the words they spoke. "Glad you made it back OK."

The twins stretched out on the floor while Nate and Harry sat at a dusty old dining table that may have at one time, long ago, been surrounded by the sounds of happy children eating breakfast. Bonesteel relaxed on a makeshift bed made of old rags and blankets. They rested, laughed, reviewed the escapades of the afternoon, and filled each other in on their encounters with the enemy. As the afternoon light began to fade, only one man was missing. "Has anybody seen O'Banyon?" Ezra asked.

"Last I saw him, he was talking to some horses," Carlos said.

"Typical Irishman," Bonesteel said with disdain.

"He's probably off somewhere dancing an Irish gig," Harry Whitecloud offered.

"Do you mean an Irish jig?" Roberto howled.

"Gig. Jig. However you white men say it," Harry answered. The other men chuckled at Harry's mistake. Educated in some of the finest schools in the Northeast, Harry nonetheless occasionally made a mess of his adopted language. When he did, the twins were quick to let him know it.

"Hard telling where that free spirit might have wandered off to," Carlos said as he shook his head and grinned. "If he was enjoyin' the scenery, he might be halfway to Richmond by now."

"Especially if someone told him there was a Blarney stone in that direction!" laughed Roberto. "Wherever he went, he better get back here pretty soon, or he's gonna be all alone out there behind enemy lines."

"Naah, O'Banyon's never really alone," said Nate, his lips turning into a smile. "The Lord's with him and watchin' out for him."

"I sure hope so," Ezra said.

A FEW MINUTES LATER, the men in the cabin heard a horse neighing outside in the woods. Then another.

"Cover the windows!" Ezra commanded. "Reginald, take the front door." The men were already pulling their carbines while Ezra barked rapid-fire orders in a firm but quiet whisper. "Carlos and Roberto, get upstairs. Nate, cover the back door. Nobody fire until I do."

Sounds of several snorting horses could be heard thrashing through the brush outside, their riders making no attempt to conceal their actions. Justice increased the pressure on the LaMat's trigger.

"Wait. Don't shoot!" Carlos called from upstairs. "It's O'Banyon! And he has half a dozen horses with him, as well."

"What?" Ezra looked out the window and saw Shaun O'Banyon approaching the cabin with five or six horses in tow. Justice couldn't believe that Shaun would jeopardize his life to bring the horses through the thick woods to safety. But that was the kind of man Shaun O'Banyon was. Always thinking about how he could help someone, even if the *someone* was a four-footed animal.

Ezra opened the door and went outside on the porch as O'Banyon tied the horses to a nearby tree. Justice stood on the porch, his LaMat revolver in the holster on his hip. "Shaun O'Banyon, what on earth are you doing with those horses?"

"They are such fine specimens, aren't they, Cap'n? They were much too lovely to simply let go. After all, they might mistakenly wander back to the Johnny Rebs. And we couldn't have that, now could, we?"

Ezra stepped off the porch and patted one of the stallions. "They are beautiful animals, Shaun. I'm just not sure what we're gonna do with them. We already have horses. But it was good of you to save them."

"Ah, my Lizzie would have it no other way. She would wallop me sure enough, if she were thinkin' I left these beauties in the devil's hand," O'Banyon said as he pulled a small locket out of his breast pocket and flipped it open. Inside was a picture of his wife, Elizabeth O'Banyon. "Lizzie loves animals of all kinds but especially these big fellows. And she has just the right touch with them. She can shoe a horse better than I can." O'Banyon looked at the photo in the locket. "She's a dear one, she is." He snapped the locket closed and replaced it in his jacket pocket.

With O'Banyon back in the camp, Ezra could finally relax. All of the men loved Shaun O'Banyon, even Bonesteel, though the hard-nosed Brit would never admit it. Nevertheless, he maintained a grudging respect for the Irish O'Banyon as a courageous soldier, a man willing to lay down his life for his brothers, and as a man of utmost integrity.

O'Banyon nearly drove Ezra crazy at times with his rambunctious behavior, but Justice saw the good in O'Banyon and loved him as his own brother. Shaun O'Banyon was one of the first men Justice had recruited. Ezra sat down on the floor, leaned back against the wall, and looked around the cabin at the valiant men in his squad, each one an expert in his field. Ezra smiled as he recalled how he had brought this unusual assortment of men together.

About the Authors

CHUCK NORRIS is an internationally known movie and television star, a six-time world martial arts champion, and the founder of the World Combat League, a new sport combining karate and kickboxing skills along with unparalleled athleticism. Chuck has received numerous humanitarian awards, but he regards his most rewarding accomplishment the creation of KICKSTART, an organization working to build strong character in youth by teaching them martial arts in their schools.

KEN ABRAHAM is a *New York Times* best-selling author who has cowritten books with Chuck Norris (*Against All Odds*), Lisa Beamer (*Let's Roll!*), Tracey Stewart (*Payne Stewart: The Authorized Biography*), and numerous others.

AARON NORRIS is a movie and television producer, actor, director, and writer, a martial arts expert, and president of Norris Brothers Entertainment.

TIM GRAYEM is CEO of The Canon Group and a successful film writer.